Information Age Economy

Information Age Economy

F. Rose
The Economics, Concept, and Design
of Information Intermediaries
1999, ISBN 3-7908-1168-8

S. Weber
Information Technology in Supplier Network
2001, ISBN 3-7908-1395-8

K. Geihs, W. König and F. von Westarp (Eds.)
Networks
2002, ISBN 3-7908-1449-0

Falk von Westarp

Modeling
Software Markets

Empirical Analysis,
Network Simulations,
and Marketing Implications

With 73 Figures
and 32 Tables

Springer-Verlag Berlin Heidelberg GmbH

Dr. Falk Graf von Westarp
TMP Worldwide/Monster
Hohenstaufenstraße 7
65189 Wiesbaden
E-mail: falk@westarp.com

ISBN 978-3-7908-0009-8   ISBN 978-3-642-57377-4 (eBook)

DOI 10.1007/978-3-642-57377-4

Cataloging-in-Publication Data applied for
A catalog record for this book is available from the Library of Congress.

Bibliographic information published by Die Deutsche Bibliothek
Die Deutsche Bibliothek lists this publication in the Deutsche Nationalbibliografie; detailed
bibliographic data is available in the Internet at *http://dnb.ddb.de*.

http://www.springer.de
© Springer-Verlag Berlin Heidelberg 2003

Cover design: Erich Kirchner, Heidelberg

SPIN 10902684   88/3130-5 4 3 2 1 0 – Printed on acid-free paper

Foreword

As social beings, humans are not living in isolation but rather interact and communicate within their social network via language, meant to convey parts of some conceptualization from the sender to a single recipient or a set of recipients. Communities of agents not only share a common language but also the individual conceptualizations of the world (real and abstract) have to overlap to a significant extent, allowing for efficient reference to whole conceptual structures like "the German constitution", "game theory" or "medical sciences".

For "societies" of interacting technical devices or software agents the situation is not quite as Babylonian since although these agents are meant to act individually (and also have a private state and private knowledge) in most cases they are designed to refer to *one* common ontology or standardized protocol and thus do not have to deal with misunderstanding. However, the more these systems become interconnected, the more this situation resembles the one described for societies of human agents even though the misunderstanding might be easier to detect when the different reference ontologies are made explicit and published.

Obviously, in both cases *standardization* of a common language or set of rules for interaction reduces the individual degree of freedom for the sake of compatibility and benefits derived from interaction.

In his work, Falk Graf von Westarp addresses the *software market* as a domain strongly depending on compatibility effects of the individuals' decisions.

According to *Network Effect* literature these network externalities lead to *market failure* due to Pareto-inferior coordination results. The author shows that existing models of adoption or standardization processes are not able to explain the variety of diffusion courses observable in today's dynamic IT markets and derives requirements for a more general model of network effects.

Economic theory of positive *network externalities* emphasizes that the installed base of a product determines the adoption decision of individuals in network effect markets. Structural properties of the *personal* network of communication and interaction are neglected. At the same time models of *geographical* and *sociological network analysis* consider a variety of structural properties but are unable to explain diffusion processes in presence of strong network externalities.

Supported by extensive empirical research Graf von Westarp integrates both approaches into a simulation model of the actual diffusion process and identifies determinants predicting its result. He shows that homogeneous preferences, low prices, high connectivity, a random "global" topology or a centralized structure of the network are likely result in market dominance of single product. In contrast, heterogeneity of preferences, high product prices and a decentralized, regional or sparse structure of the network prevent concentration.

The work makes a strong point against using macro models of some "aggregate" behavior, be it in economics or other social sciences, which is not grounded on micro-modeling of individual decision making accounting for the interdependencies with the individual's personal environment. When taking this personal context into account, a totally different system dynamics may emerge on the macro level.

Besides the fact that the new approach is a very valuable contribution for the related research fields, the author also proves the relevance for real-world decisions by providing marketing guidelines for suppliers in software markets as well as decision support for buyers.

Prof. Dr. Wolfgang König

Acknowledgements

I am indebted to many people who gave their inspiration, time and knowledge to help me with my research work.

Especially I would like to thank Prof. Dr. Wolfgang König and Prof. Dr. Peter Buxmann, who introduced me to the field of standardization and coordination in networks and who always supported me generously.

During the empirical study in the United States of America I received invaluable support from Prof. Hal Varian, Prof. Arie Segev and Dr. Judith Gebauer from the University of California, Berkeley, as well as from Linda and Tony Tyshuk, and Astrid Ruhrmann.

I am particular grateful that I had Dr. Oliver Wendt and Dr. Tim Weitzel at my side with whom I could not only share my scientific ideas but also numerous bottles of wine. These two extraordinary friends have been my inspiration in many ways, often far beyond scientific questions.

I am also indebted to the German National Science Foundation for funding my research, which was part of the interdisciplinary research program "Networks as a competitive advantage".

Dr. Falk Graf von Westarp

Contents

1 Introduction

1.1 Modern Software Markets

With an estimated volume ranging from $114 billion (WITSA 1998) to $300 billion dollars (Gröhn 1999, 23) in 1997, the software market is one of today's most important world markets.

Daily success stories of young companies with skyrocketing stocks (recent examples include Ariba, Commerce One, and Intershop) illustrate the dynamics and innovativeness of the software market. Another recent example is the emergence of innovations like the new Internet standard XML and various related products. The World Wide Web Consortium (W3C) recommended this standard in February 1998 and about a year later it already experienced a dramatic acceptance with all large software vendors planning to develop new products with extended functionality.

Besides a high momentum in technical innovations and strong competitiveness in software markets, leading to constantly shorter product cycles and even higher pressure towards innovativeness, one can also identify paradigm shifts that lead to fundamental changes of business rules in general.

The trend towards standardized products and the trend towards networked computer systems are two important shifts in the evolution of modern software markets.

Standardized products are characterized by high costs for producing the first copy but, in contrast to custom-made solutions, low (or nearly negligible) costs for producing additional copies. This cost structure has important implications. Because of cheap and easy reproduction (in this context referred to as *instant scalability*) a product which is recognized by consumers as superior can quickly be offered in sufficient quantities to satisfy the entire market. Pricing is also completely independent of marginal production costs, resulting in the need for new pricing strategies. Compatibility is another characteristic of standardized products that has gained in importance in recent years. An example of market changes due to the trend towards standardization is the success of Microsoft with a 2,790% increase in profit and a 1,665% increase in revenue between 1990 and 1999. Another example is the ongoing shift from traditional (mostly custom-made) EDI to standardized WebEDI solutions that might lead to other stories of this kind with yet unknown players.

The shift from stand-alone to *networked computer systems* has other important implications for software markets. Nearly every computer in today's world is part of or connected to some kind of communication network. The growth of the Internet for example is proceeding with such breathtaking speed that it makes figures obsolete within a few months.[1] In this networked world important benefits of software derive from the ability to exchange data or information between different system components or different systems. Users can be seen as participants of communication networks within which it is fundamental that communication partners use compatible software standards and therefore coordinate the use of their individual technology. The need for compatibility leads to the phenomenon of strong positive consumption interdependencies which are referred to as *demand-side economies of scale* or *positive network effects*. What does this mean for the dynamics in software markets? In markets with strong positive network effects, potential buyers might hesitate to adopt an innovation since they fear being stranded with a technology which might not be able to attract the *critical mass* to become the new de facto standard. In that case, early adopters might be forced to switch to another more successful product bearing the resulting *switching cost*. In contrast, once a product reaches the critical point in diffusion, the product might experience explosive growth. The Internet is a good example of such technologies which were developed in the late 1960s. When it finally took off in the early 1990s, the rapid success took some of the largest software vendors by surprise, who as a result quickly had to invest hefty sums of money to avoid competitive disadvantages.

1.2 Research Motivation

Looking at such dynamic changes in markets that did not even exist a few decades ago, and at the same time observing their growing importance in today's private and business life, the question arises whether existing economic models are capable of explaining and forecasting relevant phenomena in order to help vendors and buyers to make the right strategic decisions.

---

[1] Most recent numbers of Internet users are: 16 million in 12/1995 (0.39% of the world population), 304 million in 03/2000 (5.0%), 333 million in 06/2000 (5.4%), Nua Internet Surveys, Nua Ltd., http://www.nua.ie.

In this context, it must be the objective of economic approaches to provide answers to relevant questions on both sides of the market. Existing suppliers need appropriate models to develop strategies to keep or extend the market shares of their existing software products or whether to enter new markets or market segments. Newcomers (such as Ariba, Commerce One, or Intershop) need advice on *how* to explore *what* markets (often with the help of large amounts of investment money due to their enormous market capitalization, Ariba for example has a market capitalization of $23 billion and Intershop of $5.6 billion). Finally, potential buyers need help in making the right decisions about software by choosing the right supplier in terms of product quality and in terms of not getting stranded with a technology which will later fail to be sufficiently adopted in the market. Additionally, buyers of software solutions seek advice on how to coordinate compatibility within their own communication network by collectively or individually choosing the appropriate software.

Existing economic approaches, e.g. from *marketing* or *diffusion theory*, *standardization research*, or *network effect theory*, are not able to provide appropriate support to solve these decision problems. In the following some examples of "old economy" concepts are given that have to be reconsidered to take the fundamental paradigm shifts that lead to a "new (information) economy" into account.

Positive network effects imply that individual demand is not only dependent on the attributes and the price of a good but also on the demand of other consumers. This leads to the situation that the demand curve for an entire market cannot any longer be horizontally aggregated. Therefore, it cannot be described as a function of the price alone. To determine the aggregate demand curve, the demand would already have to be known, a circle which is difficult to overcome (Leibenstein 1950, Rohlfs 1974, Wiese 1990).

A known restriction of the neo-classical paradigm is the divisibility of goods. While this assumption is already questionable for the old economy, it becomes even more inappropriate for a new economy which emphasizes the relevance of information goods for which the optimum quantity of an individual's demand is one.

Due to extreme production side economies of scale (the cost of reproduction are very small) and due to network effects on the demand side, software markets have a propensity to monopolize. In the old economy this implies the danger of misuse of monopoly power (restricting output, raising prices) to capture monopoly rents. In the new economy, even in monopolized markets software prices are constantly dropping (see section 3.4) and, for example, because of instant scalability, monopolies are under constant pressure from relatively small players, (e.g. Microsoft sees Linux and related applications as a serious threat to its market position).

1.3   Research Objective

The objective of this work is to identify the relevant determinants of modern software markets, and to incorporate these in a simulation model providing the basis for an integrated theory of software markets and for managerial directions for software vendors to develop and implement strategies in a new economy.

To reach this goal, an analysis will be conducted of how far the existing theoretical and empirical approaches consider real world phenomena in modern software markets. An agent-based simulation model will be developed which integrates useful traditional concepts with this new approach to model the software market as a relational diffusion network.

The focus of this work will be on software which is used for data manipulation, storage, and/or transmission in the corporate world. To gain insights into market phenomena and to identify different instances of general market determinants the market for enterprise resource planning systems (like SAP R/3 or Peoplesoft), the market for EDI solutions and the market for office communication applications (like MS Office or Lotus Smart Suite) will be empirically analyzed and compared.

1.4   Structure of the Thesis

Figure 1 gives an overview of the structure of the thesis. Besides an introductory description of the common characteristics and phenomena of software markets (chapter 2), this work consists of a combination of three different research approaches, empirical analysis (chapter 3), evaluation of existing models from different research fields (chapter 4 and 5), and simulations (chapter 6 and 7).

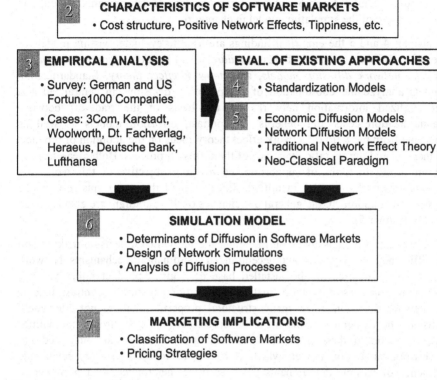

Figure 1: Structure of the thesis.

In chapter 2 common characteristics of software markets and concepts describing these are introduced. Besides cost structure, instant scalability, and pricing, phenomena like positive network effects, tippiness, start-up problems, critical mass, and the propensity to monopolization are described. Since there is an overflow of classifications and concepts concerning software (e.g. software as an experience good, Shapiro/Varian 1998, 5-6, software as an investment good, Baaken/Launen 1993, or welfare implications of network externalities in software markets, Gröhn 1999), only the characteristics that are relevant in the context of this work are listed.

Chapter 3 consists of an empirical study using the Fortune1000 companies in Germany and the United States as well as case studies with large German and American companies. The studies aim at analyzing the corporate behavior concerning the choice, adoption, and use of products in the markets of ERP systems, EDI solutions, and office communication software. The differences between the three markets, particularly in terms of market structure, price segment, role of network effects and compatibility, and preferences towards compatibility, are identified. These will later build the basis for evaluating existing concepts in chapter 4 and 5 and for identifying typical determinants of adoption for the design of the simulation model in chapter 6.

In chapter 4 and 5 the empirical findings are used to evaluate existing models of the four different research fields *standardization models, economic diffusion models, network diffusion models,* and *network effect theory.* Standardization models analyze the coordination of compatibility decisions in centralized and decentralized information networks on the basis of the trade-off between standardization costs and benefits. In contrast, diffusion models as well as concepts from the field of network effect theory focus on the adoption of products in markets and the specific dynamics of the diffusion process. Both areas seem to be promising in terms of supporting the research objective of this work, but serious drawbacks are also identified. Since most of these concepts rely on the neo-classical approach, the general deficiencies of this paradigm are also revealed (end of chapter 5).

Standardization models focus on modeling the individual's decision-making and the efficiency of centralized and decentralized coordination mechanisms. Network effect theory focuses on the installed base of a given product rather than on structural properties of the individual communication network. In contrast, models of network diffusion cover many structural properties, but do not adequately consider the dynamics of the diffusion process itself when strong externalities exist. In section 6, these approaches and the empirical findings are integrated into a network simulation model, which is then used to systematically reveal the influence of various determinants (such as price, heterogeneity of preferences, connectivity, centrality, and topology of networks) on diffusion processes in software markets.

Chapter 7 applies the simulation results to a marketing context. Here, software markets are classified in terms of their tendency to monopolize and in terms of their stability. Different vendor roles are derived for these markets implying different marketing strategies. Furthermore, additional simulations are conducted to analyze competitive pricing strategies in software markets with different market structures. Again, recommendations for vendors in the different markets are given.

Since this new approach to modeling software markets as a relational diffusion network is seen as a framework for further research in the area of software markets and diffusion processes in networks, some possible directions for future research are shown in chapter 8. A promising extension of the simulation model seems to be a further integration with the decentralized standardization model to test how different designs of individual decision-making influence diffusion processes in software markets. Additionally, the design of new measures which reflect real world topologies and which at the same time can be used to systematically generate artificial networks seems to be beneficial for research into diffusion networks. While a great variety of measures exists to classify networks by using empirical data sets, measures for generating networks (e.g. of a certain centrality) are still not sufficiently explored. The model can be applied to analyzing and forecasting the dynamics of software diffusion in real world networks. Therefore, preliminary work on methods for the collection of empirical data of relevant communication networks (such as business networks) is described.

2 Characteristics of Software Markets

In this section characteristics and phenomena of the software markets that distinguish software markets from traditional markets will be described.

Cost structure: It is costly to produce the first copy of a software product while the costs of additional copies are very low (e.g. CD-ROM) or even negligible (e.g. if distributed via download from the Internet). In economic terms this means high fixed costs and very low marginal costs leading to substantial economies of scale (Shapiro/Varian 1998, 20-22). Since software is immaterial, the distribution costs are also significantly lower than for physical goods. Even very large programs fit on a single CD-ROM or can easily be downloaded over the Internet. With increasing bandwidth and with the offering of flat rates by Internet Service Providers the latter is expected to increase further.

Instant scalability: Closely related to the cost structure is the phenomenon of instant scalability in software markets. Since it is so easy to reproduce and distribute copies of software, suppliers can respond very quickly to an increase in demand. Therefore, once a software product is recognized as superior, the particular vendor might be able to gain significant market share in a very short time period (Liebowitz/Margolis 1999, 137).

Pricing: Cost structure and instant scalability influence pricing strategies in software markets. Of course it does not make sense to apply cost-based pricing if the costs of reproduction are close to zero. On the one hand, pricing is more likely to be determined by consumer value, leading to *differential pricing* (Shapiro/Varian 1998, 37-51). Because of the importance of the installed base due to positive network effects on the demand side of the market, dynamic pricing (and in particular *penetration pricing*) is one of the most important strategies in modern software markets. Appropriate pricing strategies for different market types will be explored in section 7 of this work).

Positive network effects: It is common in many markets for the buying decision of one consumer to influence the decisions of others. Interdependencies such as the *bandwagon, snob,* and *Veblen effect* are broadly discussed in economic literature (e.g. Leibenstein 1950, Ceci/Kain 1982). Besides these general effects, which apply to all consumer decisions, software markets are determined by strong *positive network effects*, the so-called *demand-sided economies of scale*, deriving from the need for product compatibility. This means that the willingness to adopt a product innovation correlates positively with the number of existing adopters. These effects mainly originate from two different areas, the need for compatible products to exchange data or information (*direct network effects*) and the need for complementary products and services (*indirect network effects*) (Katz/Shapiro 1985, Economides 1996b). The role of different types of network effects in comparison to price and product attributes will be examined in the empirical studies of section 3. Which other determinants might influence network effects and their impact on diffusion processes in software markets will be analyzed in section 6. Since the early approaches to analyzing demand-side interdependencies in the telecommunication market (Rohlfs 1974, Oren/Smith 1981), there has been a broad discussion of positive network effects in economic literature (e.g. Dybvig/Spatt 1983, Kindleberger 1983, Katz/Shapiro 1985, Farrell/Saloner 1985, Katz/Shapiro 1986, Farrell/Saloner 1986, Katz/Shapiro 1992). In section 5.2, a comprehensive analysis of this research field, referred to as the *theory of positive network effects*, will be conducted.

Tippiness: Supply-sided economies of scale, instant scalability, and positive network effects can result in a specific dynamic structural change in software markets referred to in literature as *tippiness*. If the diffusion of a certain software product gains sufficient momentum the market might tip meaning that at the expense of its competitors the particular product takes over the entire market in a short time. While many approaches in network effect theory analytically analyze the phenomenon of tipping in network effect markets (e.g. Besen/Farrell 1994, Katz/Shapiro 1985), Liebowitz and Margolis (1999) have recently criticized this concept based on empirical studies of office communication software, browsers and other standard applications. Based on the simulations in section 6 the new model of market classification in section 7 will distinguish between stable and unstable (tippy) software market types.

Start-up problem and critical mass: When a good has little or no value without other users a *start-up problem* occurs. Because of the relevance of network effects, early adopters bear the risk of buying a product which might not succeed in gaining the expected market share. This can lead to *excess inertia* even if the product is seen as superior (e.g. Katz/Shapiro 1985, 1994, Wiese 1990, Besen/Farell 1994, Economides/Himmelberg 1995). Related to the start-up problem is the *critical mass*, being the critical number of users needed to overcome the start-up problem. Reaching this point in the diffusion process might then again result in rapid acceleration and in the tipping of the market.

Propensity to monopolize: Network effect literature states that multiple, incompatible technologies can only rarely coexist in markets with high supply- and demand-sided economies of scale, and instant scalability resulting in a tendency to monopolize. Empirical observations show monopolistic structures in some of the modern software markets like the market for office suites, word processors, or spreadsheets (Gröhn 1999, Liebowitz/Margolis 1999). Whether this is a phenomenon of software markets in general and what might be the relevant characteristics leading to differences in market concentration will comprehensively be analyzed in section 6 and 7.

3 Empirical Analysis of Software Markets

The focus of this chapter is on the empirical analysis of corporate behavior concerning the choice, adoption, and use of software products for data manipulation, storage, and/or transmission. Examples of this behavior are given for the software categories Enterprise Resource Planning (ERP) systems (or more generally: business software), Electronic Data Interchange (EDI), and office communication software (word processors, spreadsheets, etc.). To collect empirical data for the analysis a comprehensive empirical survey was conducted in Germany and the US. The results on a general level were complemented by case studies which give examples demonstrating the specific behavior of individual German and US companies.

3.1 Design of the Empirical Study

The survey was conducted in the summer of 1998. A questionnaire containing about 30 questions on 8 pages (see appendix A) was sent to 1000 of the largest companies both in Germany and the United States. For the US sample the 1998 Fortune1000 companies database was used (www.fortune1000.com). In Germany the 1000 largest companies were determined by using a list of the largest 500 companies (Schmacke 1997) which was completed by the 1998 database of the Schoder Direct Marketing GmbH&Co, Ditzingen, from which the largest companies by the number of employees were taken. Prior to mailing the questionnaire, each company was contacted by phone to identify the head of the MIS department to whom the questionnaire was then directly addressed. The respondents had the choice between filling out the paper version of the survey and sending it back by mail or the use of an online web-based survey form. 250 completed questionnaires were returned in Germany (25%), and 102 in the US (10.2%). SPSS was used for the data analysis.

The general research questions of the survey can be summarized as follows:

- Which IT standards do companies currently use and which will they use in the future?

- How significant are the problems of incompatibility for different categories of software?

- Who are the decision-makers for the adoption and implementation of IT standards in enterprises?

- What are the potential advantages and disadvantages of centralizing the management of software standards?

- How relevant are various criteria like price, functionality, market penetration, pressure from business partners, etc. for decisions on software products?

On the one hand, the study was designed to provide an insight into the determinants of strategic standardization issues like the diversity of software solutions, compatibility problems, and the centralization of decision structure. On the other hand, more detailed questions are asked for the selected categories *Enterprise Resource Planning (ERP) systems*, *EDI solutions*, *office communication software* and *Internet technology*. The latter will not be discussed in this work (see Westarp/Buxmann/Weitzel/König 1999 for further results in this area). Figure 2 shows the structure of the questionnaire.

General questions
- variety of solutions within different categories
- problems of compatibility
- pros and cons of centrally specifying standards

ERP systems (business software)	EDI	Office communication	Internet technology
- products used - proportion of custom-made software - selection criterions - decision makers - opinion on some general statements	- standards used - reasons for implementation - selection criterions - make or buy of EDI services - costs and benefits - decision makers - Internet-based EDI	- products used - selection criterions	- areas of use Internet/Intranet: - central/decentral decision on content - central/decentral data entry

Personal opinions of the MIS managers on general statements

Demographic data of participating enterprises

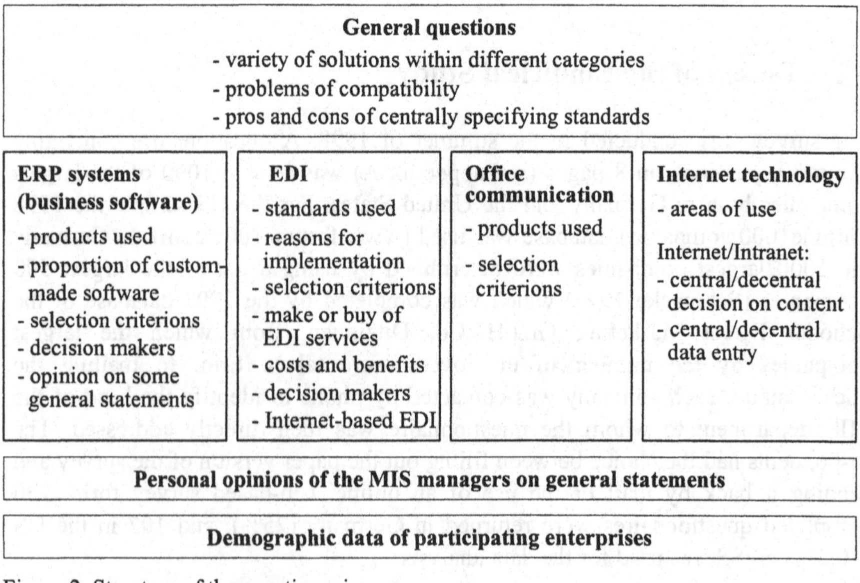

Figure 2: Structure of the questionnaire.

Looking at the demographic characteristics of the samples, the German sample is dominated by manufacturing (38%) followed by retail (16%), financial services and insurance (10%), other services (10%), energy and water supply (6%), transportation and communication (6%), construction (4%), and health care and social services (3%) (Figure 3). Of the 94 participants that belong to the manufacturing sector, 21 are from the engineering industry (8.4% of the full sample), 18 from the automobile industry (7.2%), and 14 from the chemical industry (5.6%).

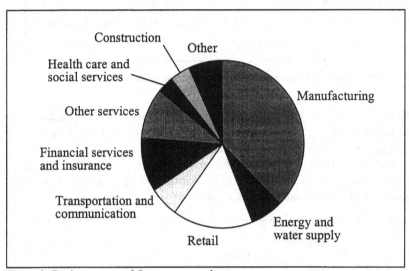

Figure 3: Business areas of German respondents.

Figure 4 shows the annual national revenues[2] and the number of employees for the different sectors of the responding German companies.

---

2   Whenever figures of German DM in this work were transformed into US $, the rate of $1 = DM1.7 was used.

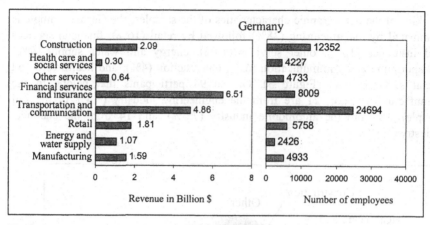

Figure 4: Average size of German enterprises responding in each sector.

Like the German sample, the US sample with 102 respondents is also dominated by manufacturing (43%). The other participants belong to retail (14%), financial services and insurance (9%), transportation and communication (9%), health care and social services (6%), energy and water supply (5%), other services (4%), and mining (4%) (Figure 5). The companies in the manufacturing sector belong mainly to the food, oil, chemical, and electronics industries.

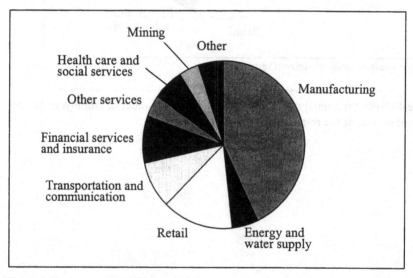

Figure 5: Business areas of US respondents.

Figure 6 shows the annual national revenues and the number of employees for the different sectors of the responding US companies.

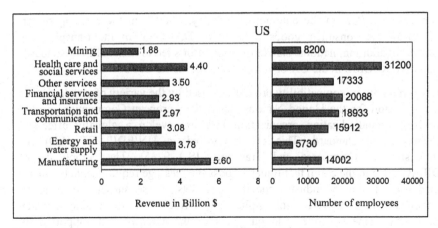

Figure 6: Average size of US enterprises responding in each sector.

Generally, the companies in the US sample are far larger in terms of national revenue and the number of employees. The only exceptions to this are the sectors financial services and insurance, and transportation and communication.

In the following, the specifics of the software market will be characterized by empirical analysis of the decision process, the role of different types of network effects, the specifics of the use, and the costs and benefits of the products. The results will be used for evaluating centralized and decentralized standardization models in section 4, and diffusion models and network effect theory in section 4. They will also build the basis of the network diffusion simulation in section 6.

3.2   The Status Quo and the Future of EDI Systems

3.2.1   Traditional EDI

Electronic Data Interchange (EDI) is the business-to-business exchange of electronic documents in a standardized machine-processable format. EDI enables partners to electronically exchange structured business documents, such as purchase orders and invoices, between their computer systems. In contrast to traditional paper-based transactions there is no human intervention. Data is automatically generated in one computer system and sent to another to be processed automatically.

Prior to exchanging EDI documents, partners must first agree on a common standard to structure the content of the documents, i.e. the EDI standard. The content of the transmitted documents varies in respect of the industry concerned. Therefore a variety of industry specific EDI standards has emerged over the years.

Examples are VDA in the automotive industry, SWIFT in the banking sector, SEDAS in the consumer goods industry or DAKOSY in the transportation industry. In addition, national standardization efforts led to national EDI standards like TRADACOMS in the UK or ANSI ASC X12 in the USA.

The overcoming of compatibility problems caused by the variety of standards was the motivation for the United Nations (UN), the European Community and the worldwide standardization organization ISO to develop a globally effective, industry-neutral standard. This effort resulted in UN/EDIFACT (EDI for Administration, Commerce and Transport, ISO 9735). The complexity of EDIFACT due to the claim that it met all possible message requirements led to so-called - again mostly industry specific - subsets. These subsets are a 'small solution' or an 'EDIFACT light' application, a fraction of the usable message types, data elements, codes and qualifiers of the extensive set supported by EDIFACT. Subsets only employ that small part of the large amount of EDIFACT messages the particular user really utilizes. Therefore, from a user's perspective, subsets are often more efficient since their implementation is considerably more cost-effective. This led to industry-specific EDIFACT subsets like ODETTE (Organization for Data Exchange by Teletransmission in Europe) in the automotive industry, CEFIC (Conseil Européen des Fédération de l'Industrie Chemique) in the chemical industry, EDIFICE (EDI Forum for Companies with Interests in Computing and Electronics) in the electronic industry, EDICON (EDI Construction) in the construction industry or RINET (Reinsurance and Insurance Network) in the insurance industry.

The cost and time savings resulting from using EDI can be considerable. Direct savings result from decreased information costs due to cheaper and faster communication. Additionally, avoiding media discontinuities eliminates the errors that occur due to re-keying of data or reformatting of documents. The immediate availability of the data allows an automation and coordination of different business processes, e. g. enabling just in time production. As a result, an enterprise can reduce its stocks drastically, capital investment in stocks decreases; it can react faster to changes in its competitive environment. Often, administrative overheads can be reduced and unnecessary loss of information can be avoided since enterprises do not take full advantage of all information available due to the costs of manual data input.

Another reason discussed in the literature on EDI why EDI is implemented in enterprises is the possibility of offering better service to customers. It is also common that smaller companies especially are forced to implement the EDI standard of the larger partner by the threat of giving up the business partnership unless this is done, sometimes described as "gun-to-the-head-EDI" (Tucker 1997).

The implementation and communication costs of an EDI solution depend on the data volume, the level of integration into business processes and the number of business partners. Implementation costs consist of costs for hard- and software, possibly for an adaptation of in-house software, external consulting and the reengineering of business processes. The costs for restructuring internal processes are difficult to quantify and are often underestimated when anticipating the implementation costs of an EDI system.

Focusing on the cost of running an EDI solution, the costs of VAN (value added network) services, are an important factor. VANs offer the communication infrastructure for the exchange of EDI documents with business partners. Since there are a great number of VAN providers, the VANs also serve as a gateway to other networks enabling communication with business partners in other VANs. The charges for using the VAN depend on the size and the frequency of the data transfers as well as the transfer time (Emmelhainz 1993, 113-116).

Since the first EDI implementations in the late 1960s, companies are increasingly aware of the strategic importance of EDI for business-to-business communication. However, EDI is not as widespread as many had expected. It is estimated that nowadays only 5% of all companies who could benefit from EDI actually use it (Segev/Porra/Roldan 1997), mainly due to the considerably high costs of implementing the EDI system and for VAN services. In addition, there is the problem of deciding which specific EDI standard to implement and thereby being incompatible to other standards. Thus, there is uncertainty about which EDI standard to use since companies are afraid of being locked into a standard that is expensive to change (Buxmann/Weitzel/König 1999).

With the fast evolution of IT, the increase of interest surrounding the Internet, tendencies toward deregulation in the telecommunication markets and stronger global competition, EDI needs to be reevaluated. Due to the possibility of economizing on setup and communication costs, more and more companies consider using the Internet for their EDI communications.

The results of the empirical study with the Fortune1000 companies show that about 52% of the enterprises that responded in Germany and about 75% in the US use EDI technology to transfer structured business data. On average, German enterprises use EDI with 21% of their business partners, while it is 30% in the US. With these business partners 38% of the revenue is realized in Germany and 40% in the US. This confirms the hypothesis that EDI is primarily applied with important business partners. It also seems that EDI generally plays a more important role in the United States than in Germany.

Enterprises that want to use EDI have to choose from a variety of different standards to structure the content of the documents. The respondents were asked which particular standards are in use in their companies. Figure 7 and Figure 8 illustrate what percentage of the responding companies uses the relevant EDI standards.

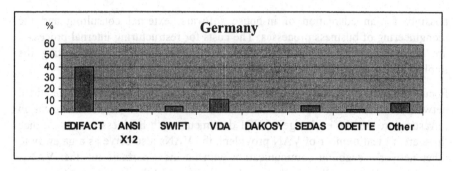

Figure 7: The use of EDI standards in Germany.

EDIFACT is by far the most popular EDI standard in Germany. It is used by nearly 40% of the responding enterprises. Other common standards follow long way behind. About 11% of the responding German companies use VDA, 6% use SEDAS, 5% use SWIFT, 3% use ODETTE, only 2% use ANSI X12, and about 1% use DAKOSY. Despite the strong position of EDIFACT, the survey reveals a marked heterogeneity in the use of EDI with many different industry-specific standards.

This heterogeneity of EDI standards was not found in the United States. The leading US EDI standard is ANSI X12 (more than 48%) followed by EDIFACT (24%). Only two of the responding enterprises in the US use SWIFT or TRADACOMS, respectively.

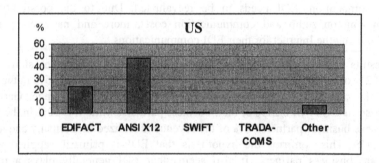

Figure 8: The use of EDI standards in the US.

These numbers only offer a static snapshot of the use of different EDI standards. To show the diffusion process over the past 14 years the respondents were also asked when they implemented their EDI solutions and if they plan changes in the future.

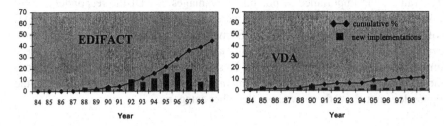

Figure 9: Diffusion of EDI standards in Germany.

Figure 9 shows the diffusion process of the two most common standards in Germany. The number of new implementations and the cumulative percentage of users is shown for every year since 1984. The * symbol shows the number of respondents who plan to use the particular standard in the near future. The success story of EDIFACT is very obvious. While VDA shows a small linear growth with comparably low rates of increase in the 90s, the use of EDIFACT is growing exponentially. Taking into account those enterprises who plan to use EDIFACT, this standard will soon reach a diffusion of nearly 44% among large companies in Germany.

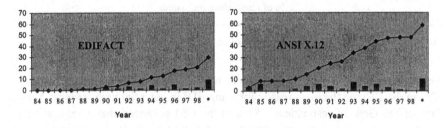

Figure 10: Diffusion of EDI standards in the US.

Figure 10 displays the diffusion of the two most common EDI standards in the US, EDIFACT and ANSI X12. If one focuses on the curves without the number of enterprises that plan to implement these standards in the future it appears that the diffusion process of ANSI X12 is slowing down significantly. While rather high rates of increase can be observed between 1989 and 1995, the rates have been decreasing in the recent years. The curve remains stable at a high level of about 48%. In contrast, EDIFACT does not seem to have reached its peak yet. The rates of increase in 1996 and 1998 are higher (and equal in 1997) than those of ANSI X12. Taking into account the enterprises who plan to use EDI, the figures show further potential concerning both of the standards with an expected diffusion rate of up to 59% for ANSI X12 and 29% for EDIFACT.

To evaluate the importance of potential advantages of EDI the respondents were asked how important selected reasons were for the decision to implement an EDI solution in their company. The MIS managers of the EDI-using companies evaluated the reasons by using a five-category scale with the extremes "very important" and "unimportant". Figure 11 shows how often the respondents chose the categories "very important" and "important". For reasons of simplification, the figure does not show the answers in the other categories.

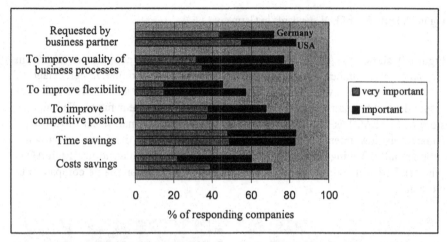

Figure 11: Reasons for the implementation of an EDI solution.

The vast majority of the MIS managers who responded (83% in Germany and 82% in the US) see the main reason for using EDI in potential time savings. About 71% of the German respondents (83% in the US) answered that a request from business partners was very important or important for their decision to implement EDI. This shows the strong influence of the individual business network on EDI decisions. The improvement of business processes was similarly important (77% in Germany and 81% in the US). Surprisingly, costs savings is not the most important argument for implementing EDI. Only 60% of the respondents in Germany and 70% in the US consider this advantage important or very important. Comparing the two countries shows that US MIS managers generally evaluate the advantages of EDI higher than their German colleagues, which corresponds to the fact that the use of EDI is more common in the United States.

The survey also determined to what extent selected EDI services are provided in-house or are outsourced. The respondents could choose from a scale with five categories and the extremes "exclusively provided in-house" and "exclusively outsourced". Table 1 shows the results, which were aggregated for reasons of simplification.

Table 1: Outsourcing of EDI services in German and US companies.

% of responding companies which use EDI	exclusively or mostly **provided in-house**		exclusively or mostly **outsourced**		both equally	
	Ger.	US	Ger.	US	Ger.	US
pure data transmission	40.9	52.9	40.2	34.3	18.9	12.9
data security (authenticity, integrity, confidentiality)	58.3	62.3	27.5	14.4	14.2	23.2
format transformation (from your format to the format of the business partner)	47.8	78.5	37.6	10	14.5	11.4
format transformation (from the format of the business partner to your own format)	53	75.3	30.7	13	16.2	11.6

The companies responding in both countries are more likely to provide EDI services in-house. This tendency is far stronger in the US than in Germany. Data security services and format transformation are exclusively or mostly outsourced only in 10 to 15% of responding companies from the US. A possible explanation for this is the fact that companies in the US sample are much larger and therefore more likely to have in-house resources like a separate EDI department. In both countries data transmission is more often outsourced than other services.

Finally, the participants that use EDI were asked about the costs and cost savings. Table 2 and Table 3 show the results for both countries.

Table 2: Costs of the company-wide implementation of the EDI solution.

	Germany	US
internal personnel time in person-hours (person months)	2400 (15)	20350 (127)
costs of software and hardware in $	167,000	201,000
costs of staff training in $	13,000	33,000
costs of external consulting services in $	71,000	54,000
other costs in $	39,000	-

Table 3: Annual costs to run the EDI solution company-wide.

	Germany	US
internal personnel costs for running and servicing the EDI solution: in $	68,000	224,000
communication costs (telephone, network, etc.) in $	59,000	75,000
annual expenses for EDI service provider in $	48,000	158,000

Table 4: Annual savings.

	Germany	US
cost savings per year in $	208,000	3,218,000

Costs and savings are significantly smaller in Germany than in the US. This is not surprising since the responding companies in the German sample are much smaller than those from the US. Nevertheless, it is unlikely that the difference in size explains the very high differences concerning the manpower needed for implementation and concerning annual cost savings. It is more likely that it results from a sample that is too small. These questions were completed only by a relatively small number of participants in both countries. The data shows that in this small sample the costs and savings that derive from using EDI solutions vary extremely among the different companies. For instance, the over all savings in the US have a range from 100,000$ to 20,000,000$, while at the same time between

100 and 250,000 person-hours were needed to implement the solution. Faced with such extreme heterogeneity with very different situations in different companies, one comes to the conclusion that it is sensible to analyze the costs and savings in the area of EDI further by studying single companies as cases (see section 3.2.3-3.2.5).

3.2.2 The Future: WebEDI

There are significant signs that the market for EDI solutions is going to change dramatically. Traditional EDI suppliers were building complex systems which in most cases only supported one EDI standard. Most of the costs derived from customizing the products in order to integrate them with the systems of the users and those of their communication partners. Therefore standardization of the products was possible only in a limited way. Driven by the Internet and the new technologies surrounding it, new products are emerging. They offer the chance to take advantage of the benefits of electronic business-to-business communication at a fraction of the costs. But beside the cost savings, another aspect is of great importance. Traditionally, EDI solutions are tied to one specific EDI standard, and the support of different standards is very costly. This led to the fact that companies were locked into EDI standards rather than into supplier-specific standards like those in the area of ERP systems or office communication software. This might change in the near future. The low cost of the required Internet technology combined with a much greater flexibility and higher functionality through new data standards like the Extensible Markup Language (XML) (Peat/Webber 1997) facilitates the support of multiple EDI standards (Weitzel/Buxmann/Westarp 2000). Increased independence from data structures will allow greater flexibility in the exchange of structured data. This may contribute to a reduced risk of undesired lock-in situations into existing EDI standards facilitating shorter product cycles and maybe even a more frequent change of communication partners.

The results of the empirical study in 1998 confirm that many EDI systems are likely to be Internet-based in the future. While currently only 7.4% of the enterprises responding in Germany and 16.9% in the US use the Internet in some way for EDI, more than 50 per cent of the enterprises in both countries plan to do so in the future.

Based on these results, a field study was conducted to gain more information about the current and planned use of WebEDI (see appendix B). E-mails with a small questionnaire were sent out to 23 US companies from the sample that either already use or plan to use Internet-based EDI. 6 of these companies answered the questions. One of the responding companies currently uses Internet-based EDI, one was planning the implementation for the end of 1998 and the remaining four plan to use it within the next two years.

The company, which stated that it has already used Internet-based EDI since 1997 uses the Internet only for sending X12 data files as attachments to e-mails. The unencrypted documents are exchanged with two of their customers and the volume of data exchanged is about 1% in comparison to traditional EDI.

The other respondents mostly plan both online forms and automated data exchange between two computer systems. The Internet is mainly seen as a transport mechanism. Initially, WebEDI will only be implemented with very few customers and suppliers. 5 of the 6 respondents state that they want to use standard software for the solution and they are usually planning an upgrade of the existing system. The expectations concerning the future share of Internet-based relative to traditional EDI vary between 5 and 25% for the year 2000 and between 15% and 100% for the year 2005.

The data from 1998 does not yet cover the dynamics of the current market for WebEDI products. At the moment, suppliers of new business-to-business (B2B) solutions like Commerce One, Software AG, and Intershop are trying to quickly gain market share with their standardized solutions to lock users in to their technology. Observing this, it seems likely that the future of EDI lies in highly standardized software products with similar market characteristics to existing standard software. Network effects deriving from EDI standards, for which no supplier has the property rights (also called unsponsored standards, see David/Greenstein 1990), will become less important while product specific standards/formats will become more important (just as they are for existing standard software products). Since these standards are owned by a software company (sponsored standards), marketing strategies for the market of EDI software will completely change, emphasizing strategies of locking in, dynamic pricing, etc. (see section 6).

The emergence of WebEDI is not only going to change the marketing strategies of EDI suppliers. On the demand side of the market it might directly influence strategic relationships within business networks. The empirical results show the pressure of business partners as a very important reason for the implementation of EDI. As EDI becomes more ubiquitous, it will be more and more common for companies not to accept partners who are not EDI-capable (see section 3.2.3-3.2.5; Hogan 1998). The use of EDI is more likely in larger than in smaller companies and there is a tendency towards reengineering supply chains and distribution channels by exchanging smaller for larger EDI-supporting business partners. For SMEs especially, a comparably low-cost WebEDI solution can reduce entry barriers to the business networks of larger enterprises or increase the chance of remaining in existing relationships. Participating in multiple business networks or industries might also be facilitated.

3.2.3   Case Study: 3Com[3]

With over $6 billion in annual revenues, 3Com is one of the largest players in the electronics and network communications industry worldwide. Mainly driven by the request of strong US business partners 3Com implemented an EDI solution based on the ANSI X12 standard in 1995. Due to the ongoing globalization EDIFACT was additionally implemented in 1998, since a large number of international business partners use this standard. EDI decisions in general are made by the EDI Operations unit, which is part of the highly centralized IS Organization department. Within the different business units there are also EDI analysts who coordinate the interdependencies between EDI data flow and business processes decentralized.

3Com uses EDI with about 15% of its approximately 200 business partners (suppliers and distributors). Redesigning the distribution channel management the company has recently focused on larger distributors that are more likely to support EDI. This explains the fact that about 50 per cent of the company's suppliers are already EDI capable. With EDI becoming more and more a significant strategic issue for enterprises, especially in the computer industry, 3Com is trying to convince more of its business partners to use EDI; for new suppliers and distributors it is already a requirement. 3Com expects financial services for payment processes to be integrated in its EDI network within the next year.

Like many other companies, 3Com started its EDI solution based on PC technology. Because of the rapid increase in the data volume, especially driven by the recent acquisition of U.S. Robotics, the solution was moved to a Unix platform. For data transfer 3Com uses a private VAN by IBM.

Focusing on the costs of implementation four areas can be separated.

- The *start up costs* for the EDI solution were less than $25,000 (including the first year of VAN service) since already existing technical and human resources were used.

- With the growing data traffic *new EDI project implementation* took place. In establishing the EDI Operations department, new personnel were hired. The technical infrastructure was also upgraded by installing a new Unix translator for $100,000.

- The setup *of a new trading partner* for EDI at 3Com takes about 2-3 days of a programmer's work.

- A *new transaction setup* like adding a certain document to the existing set of an EDI partnership takes a programmer about 8 working days (which is rather

---

[3]   The case study was conducted with Tom Trunda, 3Com Global EDI Project Manager, 3Com.

low compared *to* an industry average of about 2 weeks), and the mapping takes about $1,140.

The annual costs of running the solution are estimated at $350,000 for personnel, $36,000 for data transmission (VAN services), and about $17,000 for additional external services, such as software license agreements and outside contracting consultants. 3Com also sets aside a significant portion of the budget for continuing education and professional conferences.

Compared to the benefits, the costs of the EDI solution seem to be quite reasonable. At 3Com, the costs of manually processing an order process are calculated at $38 compared to $1.35 using EDI. This adds up to estimated savings of $750,000 in sales order and invoice processing. Taking into account also the reduction of data entry errors, efficiency increases due to better warehouse management, and reduction of processing delays, the EDI Operations department estimates overall savings of $1.3 million. These figures are expected to increase dramatically next year since 3Com is in the middle of consolidations due to the merger with U.S. Robotics. At the moment the EDI systems of the two companies are in the process of integration.

In the future 3Com plans to use the Internet as a transport medium for EDI. Investigations with business partners are planed for the middle of 1999, soon after the current consolidation comes to an end. Besides data entry through online forms (Intra- and Extranet) automated data exchange between two computer systems based on TCP/IP will be part of the solution.

The Internet-based EDI solution is planned to be technically separated from the existing systems, and will be designed specifically to guarantee security and liability. In the future, XML might be integrated into the solution to add functionality.

3Com sees the most important advantages in saving transmission costs. Furthermore, through faster and immediate data transfer over the Internet, response time can be reduced significantly (compared to the usual batch processing in VANs).

At the moment the Internet is not yet seen as a sufficient transport medium for EDI data, mainly because of reliability problems. Nevertheless, 3Com expects that 10-15% of its EDI will be based on the Internet by the year 2000 and even 85-100% by the year 2005.

3.2.4   Case Study: Karstadt[4]

With about 200 branches, 60,000 employees, and more than $15.61 billion in revenues (1997) Karstadt AG is one of the most important companies in the German retail industry. 100% subsidiaries are, among others, Neckerman AG, Hertie GmbH, and NUR Touristic GmbH.

As early as 1984, Karstadt started to use EDI in a pilot project on the basis of SEDAS (Standardregel einheitlicher Datenaustauschsysteme), an EDI standard for the consumer goods sector. Figure 12 shows the number of EDI-partners over time.

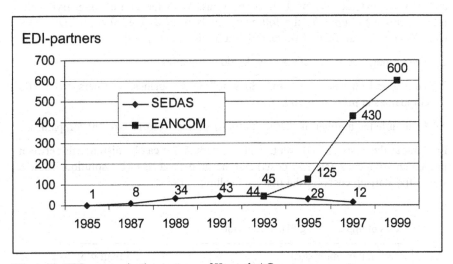

Figure 12: EDI communication partners of Karstadt AG.

The first years of EDI operation SEDAS was the only standard used. The number of business partners using it for electronic data exchange with Karstadt increased to a maximum of 44 in 1993. The introduction of the EDIFACT subset EANCOM in the same year led to a dramatic growth of EDI use. The fact that Karstadt hired external software consultants to support the effort of suppliers to implement EDIFACT additionally accelerated the increase. Up to now, around 600 or 30% of the approximately 2,000 suppliers exchange business documents with Karstadt via EDI, generating 52.2% of the annual revenues. Today, EDIFACT is the only standard in use, and while Karstadt also accepts other subsets, EANCOM is by far the most dominant. Altogether there is an electronic exchange of orders with 577 of the 600 connected companies, of delivery notes with 144 companies, of

---

[4]   The case study was conducted with Peter Niederhausen, Head of MIS (Informationswirtschaft/Warenwirtschaft), Karstadt AG, Essen.

invoices with 101 companies, of primary data with 16 companies, and of financial documents with 4 banks.

It is planned to increase the number of suppliers connected through EDI by another 20% to about 720 by 2002. At the moment, Karstadt is meeting with resistance from some business partners. These suppliers see the „slowness" of traditional communication systems as an opportunity to create a temporal buffer against strict customer deadlines. For this reason it is Karstadt's strategy to make it clear to current and potential suppliers that in future, the support of EDI will be a critical factor in the choice of business partners.

Besides trying to connect more business partners using EDI technology, Karstadt also tried to extend existing EDI connections. With the aim at intensifying the relationship with suppliers the following goals were defined for the EDI sector (for 1999) within an ECR (Efficient Consumer Response) project:

1. The homogeneous use of EAN with 300 companies.

2. To expand the use of "cross-docking" with business partners from 100 companies at present to 200.

3. To double the number of EDI users for invoicing from 100 to 200 companies.

Looking at the costs of EDI solution at Karstadt AG it can be distinguish between implementation costs (start up costs) and the running costs of the solution. Table 5 shows the start-up costs for the first EDI solution (1984).

Table 5: Costs of implementing EDI at Karstadt.

Internal personnel costs	24 man months
Soft- and Hardware	$88,200
External consulting costs	$29,400

Setting up the connection to a new supplier takes 2 to 3 man-days. These might be spread over a period of six weeks. The biggest problem is taking over primary data. Table 6 shows the annual costs of running the solution.

Table 6: Costs of running the EDI solution at Karstadt.

VAN fees	$58,800
Internal personnel costs	$35,300

There is a guideline from the company's executive board saying that new EDI projects must amortize within 18 months. Cost advantages of the use of EDI are not only direct savings concerning the transfer of data, but also general improvements in business processes on the basis of EDI. The annual savings are estimated to be between $35 million and $41 million. The following savings can be distinguished:

- Time savings: If a product is out of stock at a branch it takes only five days to make it available for customers again using EDI. Without EDI it used to take around ten days.

- There is an estimated average saving of $7 per invoice message. With 3.5 million invoices annually (1997) this results in costs savings of $24.5 million.

- In the area of order administration the savings are estimated to be 1% of the total stock value. With a stock value of $2 billion (1998) and an EDI share of 30% the annual savings add up to $6 million.

- In logistics the savings result in 1-2% of stock value. This adds up to $5.9-11.8 million.

In the near future WebEDI will play an important role at Karstadt. It is planned to fully integrate their own EDI system with those of their communication partners on the basis of XML. By the year 2010 traditional EDI is supposed to be completely replaced by WebEDI. Already in 1999 it is planned to equip 20 suppliers with an XML-prototype. Because of experiences with the large e-commerce project called "My World", the infrastructure and the know-how for implementing and running Web-based solutions already exist at Karstadt. In addition, Karstadt is an active member of the "Normenausschuß Bürowesen (NBü)", a committee of the Deutsches Institut für Normung (DIN) which is involved in the first approach to defining an XML translation table for EDI. It is foreseeable that the use of WebEDI will also involve smaller suppliers with whom communication has up to now taken place only by mail or in more urgent cases by fax.

3.2.5 Case Study: Woolworth[5]

Woolworth F. W. Co. GmbH has more than 350 branches in Germany and Austria. With its 13,000 employees it has annual revenues of more than $1.5 billion.

Woolworth implemented EDIFACT (Subset EAN-COM D 93A) in 1994. Three different document types are in use: *Order*, *Order Response*, and *Invoice*. The

---

[5]   The case study was conducted with Reinhard Sturr, Head of MIS, Woolworth F. W. Co GmbH, Frankfurt.

main reason for implementing EDI was their intention of gaining competitive advantages.

Today, approximately 3% of the 3,500 suppliers are connected with the fully integrated EDI system. The largest among them are Procter & Gamble and Herlitz, all others are medium-sized companies. Generally, suppliers are classified by relevance into A-, B-, or C-suppliers. All 105 companies which communicate with Woolworth via EDI belong to the first group. When choosing a new business partner, the selection process consists of two steps. The ability to communicate via EDI is one of the decision criteria in the second step.

The costs of implementation (start up costs) of the existing EDI solution can be distinguished as follows:

- Personnel costs: 50 man months. The main part of this time was needed to implement the converter.

- Soft- and hardware: $47,000. New computers were bought which operate on a Unix-basis.

- External services: $147,000 including $9,400 for training of employees.

- The costs of setting up a new business partner varies greatly (between three weeks and half a year) and depends on how the adjustment has to be made.

In addition the following costs occur annually:

- $42,400 for data transfer through external services. Data transfer and transformation is handled by IBM using a server located in Edingen.

- $117,700 for internal personnel costs. The EDI team, consisting of a project manager, a programmer, and a network specialist, was put together in 1994. In the future, there will be an increase in the number of staff members as it is also planned to build up consultancy competency.

The annual cost savings amount to $294,100. They can be distinguished as follows:

1. Material: reduction of fax paper, toner cartridges etc.
2. Personnel savings: it was possible to reduce the number of employees, especially in the accounting area.
3. Reduction of stock and therefore reduction of capital tie-up.
4. Time savings: the time savings can be illustrated by an example scenario (see Figure 13): When a branch (F) runs short of a certain product, a 'batch' automatically generates a physical list, which has to be checked by a supply

manager (ND) (often the orders pile up on the desk of the manager). If the list is correct, the manager sends the list to the distribution center (DC) (on average on the fourth day) where an order for the supplier (L) is generated. Using the EDI system the time was reduced to 1 - 1 ½ days. The target inventory is managed directly at the central distribution center. The supply manager only has to confirm the orders.

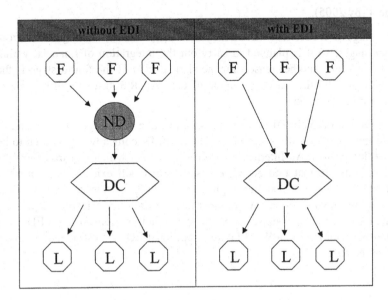

Figure 13: Exemplary order scenario with and without EDI.

To maintain the current market position a five-year plan was developed to define the next steps towards expanding EDI within the company. At the moment, this project is supervised by the management board and the MIS department. Nevertheless, the objective is to build up professional project management with representatives from every department to coordinate the different requirements.

The project consists of four stages:

- Stage 1 (by 2000):

  During this time, it is planned to reduce the number of suppliers from 3,500 to 2,000. Simultaneously business relations ought to be intensified.

- Stage 2 (by 2002):

  It is planned to switch communication with the remaining suppliers to EDI. Woolworth wants to reach this goal by transferring existing internal know-how in order to support the suppliers actively. The object is to connect approximately 1,000 to 1,200 suppliers (50 – 60%) by 2005. Occurring costs are to be split up between suppliers and Woolworth in a 'rational' manner. A split of 1/3 (supplier) to 2/3 (Woolworth) is considered.

- Stage 3 (by 2004):

  It is planned to integrate all logistic services by 2004.

- Stage 4 (by 2005):

  Up to stage 4, Woolworth will already have fundamental learning effects from earlier stages, so it is planned to carry out the integration of financial within one more year. Another reason for the short period of the fourth stage is the fact that in 2004 the banking module of the SAP R/3 system will be able to assist with integration.

The introduction of WebEDI will run parallel to these four stages. By the end of 1999, a web converter will be available. The StratEDI company was chosen to be partner of this project. An Internet-based clearing center which will transform the relevant in-house format into an XML-based format will exist. It is planned to connect the first suppliers at the beginning of 2000. In this context it is the objective of Woolworth to achieve cheaper and easier communication, especially with smaller and medium-sized suppliers. Nevertheless, conventional EDI will retain its important position. WebEDI and traditional EDI are estimated to have a future ratio of 40/60.

3.3 The Use and Management of Enterprise Resource Planning Software

This section focuses on the use and the management of ERP software. To show the variety of different solutions it will first be described which particular products are used in Germany and the United States to support business processes (including custom-made solutions). Afterwards, it will be determined which ERP-solutions are currently in use. Finally, an analysis of the centralization of the decision process on ERP-software is made, to form the basis for the analysis in section 4.

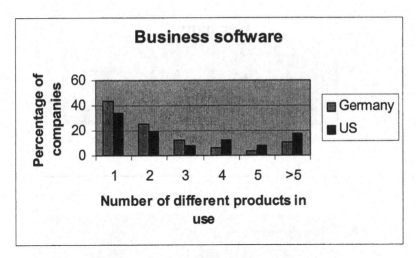

Figure 14: Number of different business software products used in the company.

Figure 14 shows that the variety of different software products used to support business processes is larger in the United States. More than 12% of the US enterprises who responded use 4 different solutions, about 8% use 5 and, even more remarkably, about 18% use more than 5 different solutions. In Germany 6% of the largest enterprises use 4 kinds of business software, 3% use 5 solutions and about 11% use more than 5 different ones.

The respondents were also asked which ERP-products are currently used in their companies. Figure 15 shows the most common ones.

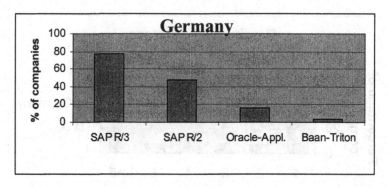

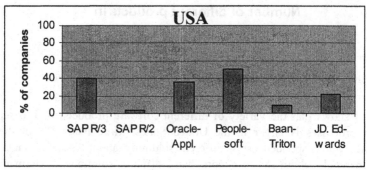

Figure 15: The most common ERP products.

The market in Germany is dominated by SAP; 77% of the respondents use R/3 and 48% use R/2. The use of competitive products is far smaller; 16% of all responding companies use Oracle-Application, and 3% use Baan Triton. In the US the market for ERP systems is much more heterogeneous. The most common products in the sample are Peoplesoft (51%), SAP (R/3: 40%, R/2: 4%), Oracle-Application (36%), J.D. Edwards (22%), and Baan Triton (9%).

3.3.1 Standardized vs. Custom-made Business Software

Besides standardized software products like SAP or Peoplesoft, the solution for the support of business processes can contain custom-made software that has been exclusively written for the individual company. The respondents were asked to estimate the proportion of standardized software in their companies. Figure 16 shows the answers.

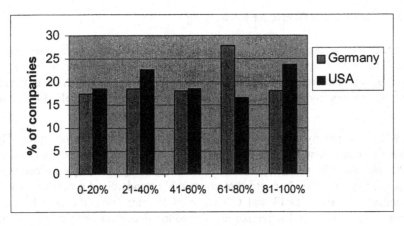

Figure 16: The proportion of standardized business software.

The answers show that there is no clear trend towards standardization or individualization respectively. On average the proportion of standard software is a little less than 50%. About as many companies are found to have very little custom-made software as companies that use very little standard software.

Focusing on that part of the solution that was custom-made, they were also asked whether this software was programmed in-house or if the programming was outsourced (Table 7).

Table 7: How was the custom-made business software predominantly produced?

in % of companies	in-house	outsourced	both equally
Germany	60.8	16.3	22.9
USA	53.8	18.7	27.5

In both countries, the custom-made part of the business software was mainly produced by internal resources of the respective company (60.8% in Germany and 53.8% in the United States). Only 16.3% of the German and 18.7% of the US companies who responded predominantly outsourced this task.

3.3.2   Case Study: Deutscher Fachverlag[6]

Deutscher Fachverlag is one of the largest independent European business press publishers with a turnover of $144 million and 760 employees in 1998. 16 subsidiaries in numerous countries publish more than 80 titles which cover twelve economic sectors and reach an annual circulation of approximately 14 million copies.

In 1984 the company implemented SAP R/2, which took about one year. The system is complemented by a large proportion of custom-made software, since SAP could not offer an adequate solution for supporting the unique processes of the publishing business. In contrast to comparably standardized processes such as accounting (the modules FI and CO are used for this task), the core business processes of Deutscher Fachverlag are the editorial content production and the management of sales, and distribution, mainly done through subscriptions. Since 1997 R/3 has been used as well as R/2. After a preparation time of 18 months, the switch to R/3 modules (FI, AM, CO, SD and MM) in certain business areas was done as a "big bang", i.e. all units switched at the same time. The migration was not used to restructure business processes; the software was simply adapted to the existing structures. The internal and external personnel costs for preparing the migration are estimated to be as follows.

Table 8: Internal and external personnel costs for preparing the migration to R/3.

	man months
Central IT unit	24
Operating departments	20
External consultants	16

The reasons for implementing R/3 in some areas were a better functionality in comparison with R/2, advantages of decentralization due to the client/server system, and the more advanced user interface. Expected compatibility problems and high costs of integrating their own custom-made publishing software with R/3 led to the decision to keep R/2 to support core business processes.

A complete migration to R/3 would have been very expensive. The different structure and syntax of R/2 and R/3 would have resulted in great difficulties in

---

6   The case study was conducted with Lutz Unkrig, Head of MIS, Verlagsgruppe Deutscher Fachverlag GmbH.

adapting a new solution to the custom-made software. The effort of developing new software was calculated to be 15 man-years.

Today, the ratio of R/3 to R/2 at the Deutscher Fachverlag is 30:70. About 220 and 100 employees are working with R/2 and R/3, respectively. Some of these are using both systems. The controlling department only uses R/3. The R/3 modules SD and MM used for organizing and invoicing workshops, selling books, and the management of stocks are of low importance. These areas contribute only 10 per cent to the total revenue. More than 80 per cent of the business is generated by subscriptions, and business magazines and advertising sales which are still supported by the custom-made publishing software and the R/2-system.

The large proportion of custom-made software shows the skepticism about reference models implemented in the ERP-solutions of SAP which are seen as not yet sufficient to deal with core processes of the publishing business. Furthermore, the decentralized business structure of the Deutscher Fachverlag, with many mostly independent publishing units, makes it very difficult to define standardized procedures which satisfy all the individual needs. Only in areas of highly standardized processes (e.g. accounting) is the decision on software centralized (in coordination with the individual business units). In other areas the units are free to choose the software which best fits their individual needs.

The SAP R/3 system is running on three servers: test server, consolidation server, and production server. The last two are Compaq Proliant servers with two Pentium 200 MHz processors each, 500 MB RAM, and 50 GB of hard disc space. The test server is less powerful. Windows NT is used as the operating system and Microsoft SQL-Server as the database.

Address database maintenance is done only with R/2 in order to guarantee data consistency and because data manipulation of R/3 in the R/2-system is feared to cause data integrity problems. Interfaces between R/2 and R/3 exist for the exchange of addresses and bookings.

The high quality but high cost support services of SAP are used intensively. During the implementation of R/3 two consultants from SAP and CSC Ploenzke were hired for 4-5 days per month each. To support the running system only one day in two months is needed.

The costs of the implementation were about $1.27 million (see Table 9).

Table 9: Costs of implementing R/3 (All figures in thousand $).

	1996	1997	1998	1999	Total
Licenses	164			12	**176**
Consulting	54	379	20		**453**
Training	41	36			**77**
Hardware	135	80			**215**
Internal IT personnel	88	132	132		**352**
Total	**482**	**627**	**152**	**12**	**1,273**

The operating costs for R/2 and R/3 add up to $1.2 million and $0.6 million per year, respectively (see Table 10).

Table 10: Operating costs for R/2 and R/3 (all figures in thousand $).

	R2	R3
Hardware (depreciation, maintenance)	191 (120, 71)	155 (141, 14)
Software	92	78
Personnel (IT department)	720	282
Consultants	42	21
Other (mainly rent and communication costs)	141	57
Total	1186	593

A comparison of costs and benefits is rather difficult since benefits are much harder to measure than costs.

3.3.3 Case Study: Heraeus[7]

The core business of the German company Heraeus is the production and processing of high-grade metals such as gold, silver and plutonium. In 1998, Heraeus had an annual net profit of $104 million and 9,594 employees worldwide

---

[7] The case study was conducted with Edmund Bechtold, Manager of Business Processes/ Customer Relationships, Heraeus infosystems GmbH.

(5,190 in Germany). The company, still owned by a single family, is subdivided into a holding company, which carries out general strategic tasks, and five independent management companies. The latter manage the operating business of all subsidiaries and associated companies, each for a certain business area (Table 11).

Table 11: Management companies and business areas of Heraeus.

management company	business area	ERP-system
W.C. Heraeus GmbH	metals, chemistry	SAP R/2 and SAP R/3
Heraeus Kulzer GmbH	dental/gems	SAP R/2 and SAP R/3
Heraeus Quarzglas GmbH	quartz glass	SAP R/2 and SAP R/3
Heraeus Electro-Nite Int. N.V.	sensors	SAP R/3
Heraeus Med GmbH	medical machines	SAP R/2

Heraeus Med GmbH only uses SAP R/2, and Heraeus Electro-Nite Int. N.V. only uses SAP R/3, all other companies use a mixture of both systems (Table 11). Around 1,000 employees work with these systems. The actual ratio of users of SAP R/2 to R/3 is 50:50. In consideration of market globalization and to guarantee the compatibility of the information systems, the existing R/2 solutions are supposed to be replaced by worldwide implementation of R/3 by 2001. Up to now, incompatible systems have held back data exchange within the Heraeus company. The implementation of SAP R/3 is only a recommendation of the holding company, since the management companies act independently and conduct their own IT projects. Heraeus Infosystems GmbH, certified by SAP as a "Customer Competence Center", usually manages the SAP implementations within the Heraeus Group while also selling this service to external customers. Infosystems also provides support when problems occur with the running of the SAP solution. In the remainder of this section the decision process about SAP R/3 and its implementation is described by presenting the case of a subsidiary of Heraeus Electro-Nite Int. N.V.

Within a three-month lead-up period, a controller and an IS expert evaluated the costs and benefits of R/3 for the subsidiary before a final decision was made. Alternatives to R/3 were either a custom-made system or a simpler standardized software to support the business processes of the company. Decisive factors for R/3 were extensive functionality, the possibility of using the system in an international environment, and transparent data representation. Pressure from an important customer of the automotive industry to meet certain requirements which could best be supported by R/3 was another critical factor. After the decision, a team consisting of 7 key users of the subsidiary and 5 employees of Heraeus

42

Infosystems implemented the solution within the scheduled 6 months. Because of this know-how it is planned to use the same team for further implementations of SAP R/3 in companies of Heraeus Electro-Nite. Table 12 shows the time table.

Table 12: Schedule for implementing R/3 at Heraeus Electro-Nite.

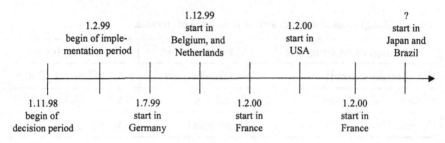

In Germany the existing R/2 solution was completely replaced by R/3. The modules FI, CO, AM, SD, MM, QM, and PP are in use. The holding uses HR, which is used in a separate SAP system.

The SAP system of the subsidiary of Electro-Nite is based on a Unix operating system and an Oracle database. The test and the consolidation system are together on one server; the production system is on a separate one in order to cut hardware costs. The servers are located at the computer center of Heraeus Infosystems. They are connected with Electro-Nite using dedicated lines. Users in the United will access the system over the Internet, as this is the most inexpensive solution for data transfer. Data security is guaranteed by firewall systems and other safety devices. The performance over the Internet seems to be adequate for the 15-20 users in the USA.

The implementation costs (in Germany) were rather low since the procedure was standardized and no custom-made programs existed. The total costs add up to $765,000 not including personnel costs of the subsidiary (see Table 13).

Table 13: Costs of implementing R/3 in Germany

Purpose	Approx. amount	Per cent
Personnel Infosystems	471,000	62 %
Hard- and software	118,000	15 %
SAP licenses	118,000	15 %
Training	59,000	8 %
Total	**765,000**	**100 %**

3.3.4   Case Study: Deutsche Bank[8]

Since Deutsche Bank took over Bankers Trust, it has been the world largest bank. Its annual surplus in 1998 was approximately DM 3.3 billion, while its balance sheet amounted to DM 1,225 billion. At the end of 1998, the number of employees came to 75,306 with approximately 65% (48,742 employees) of them working in Germany.

The Deutsche Bank is engaged in many business areas as is resembled by ist organization structure:

- Retail and Private Banking (P)
- Corporates and Real Estate (CORE)
- Global Corporates and Institutions (GCI)
- Asset Management (AM)
- Global Technology and Services

The focus of this case study will be on Deutsche Bank's SAP R/3 FI/CO-rollout. Additionally the company-wide use of SAP software will be considered.

Prior to implementing R/3 the Deutsche Bank had used SAP R/2 software since 1989 in Germany and since 1994 in Spain. Today, the ratio of R/3:R/2 usage is 80:20. It is planned to completely replace R/2 with R/3 by 2002. Otherwise, there is a uniform software solution being used but a rather heterogeneous software landscape with multiple products and a number of self-designed software programs.

---

[8]   The case study was conducted with Jos Houben, Manager of the SAP Center of Competence, Deutsche Bank AG, Frankfurt.

The major reasons for the introduction of the FI/CO-module are: globally standardized cost controlling, the use of approved controlling software, its global use in the procurement departments and the decision to outsource the development of software.

Problems like Y2K bugs and the introduction of the European currency "Euro" reinforced the need to implement a modern standardized software.

Since the structure of Deutsche Bank is changing more and more into that of a holding company, the transparency and quick availability of corporate data becomes a key success factor when purchasing and selling companies. For this reason it was planned to implement SAP R/3 at Bankers Trust right after the completion of its acquisition.

After the Deutsche Bank's decision in July 1997 to implement SAP R/3, a working R/3 architecture was set up within six months. On January 2, 1998, it was put into operation in Frankfurt and in the four most important hubs: London, Singapore, New York, and Tokyo. Altogether, this R/3-solution contained more than 200 legal entities for the module FI/CO.

By October 1999 more than twenty other branches had been equipped with SAP R/3. The Brussels and Warsaw implementations were planned to start in 1999, Sydney and Moscow following in 2000. The FI/CO-Rollout, which will have lasted 3 years altogether, including the planning process, will be finished in summer 2000.

The total time for implementing the FI/CO and MM (limited features) modules for a smaller branch like Amsterdam is estimated to take approximately 2 months utilizing a task force of two IT specialists and two advisory controllers.

In order to stay in schedule and to foster compliance for R/3 within the local staff it was required to work with a top-down decision plan and to have the complete support of the board. The SAP Center of Competence, which is associated with the department IT/Operations of Deutsche Bank, was specifically founded to support SAP projects and to manage the global implementation of SAP software in the enterprise. Individual resentment against R/3 developed because the structure of Deutsche Bank had to adapt to the software. It was necessary, for example, to adjust the controlling department to the new divisional structure of the concern and to replace regional structures.

Today most decisions regarding standardized software in the Deutsche Bank are centralized (80%), while giving a little scope to adjust to local specialties and requirements (20%). Up to now most of the the whole banking sector uses mainly custom-made software and only a few standardized solutions. But because of stricter cost control and stronger competition it is more and more necessary to take advantage of standardization potentials. Currently at Deutsche Bank the use of standardized software is less than 10 percent. This leaves plenty of room for standardized software installations.

The high number of custom-made solutions leads to difficulties in realizing the wish for transparency. In the past, critical figures were not available quickly and also were not calculated by internationally standardized formulas. This problem is solved by SAP R/3 which allows a degree of standardization that supplies the required statistics in a fast and exact mode.

The Deutsche Bank currently applies release version 4.0B of the SAP R/3 module FI/CO. The number of its users was 350 in 1997 and grew to 950 in 1998. SAP R/3 is hosted on IBM SP2 servers. The operating system is AIX, the database is supplied by Oracle.

The SAP R/3 is always being implemented with as few modifications as possible, individual design is kept to a minimum, and custom-made additions are avoided. Customization is merely done by changing a few parameters. This simplifies maintenance, updates and release changes as well as user training. In addition to the FI/CO module the following modules are in use: MM, SD, AA, EC-CS, CO-PS and HR (the "payroll" was outsourced). With IST it is also possible to use SAP R/3 in the Intranet. Because of its extended functionality the SAP has advantages over competitors like J.D. Edwards and Peoplesoft.

The necessary user-training is conducted by Deutsche Bank personnel using SAP training material.

The introduction of SAP R/3 at the Deutsche Bank was a significant investment. At the bottom line, though, it is more competitive than creating custom-made solutions. The decision for SAP R/3 is not so much based on initial costs but considered to be strategic, aiming to create a globally standardized solution.

The add-on services of SAP, like OSS, the remote-access by SAP or the Early-Watch service are used intensively and offer high quality.

In addition to SAP R/3 Peoplesoft is being used by the human resource department. Peoplesoft was implemented at the same time like R/3, in the second half of 1997. Even though a study by Andersen Consulting had concluded that SAP R/3 would be the better solution, Peoplesoft was preferred because it was already successfully in use at Deutsche Bank's branch in New York city. Yet, it was neglected that specific requirements of one branch are difficult to transfer to another.

The issue of data protection was important for SAP and thoroughly designed into the R/3 design. The concept for individual authorizations is the most extensive existing on the market right now and allows for an optimal security design. Even programmers' rights have been restricted in a way that they cannot view data while customizing SAP R/3.

Currently the IS-Banking module is being tested by the Deutsche Bank and is planned to be implemented globally in the near future.

3.4 Office Communication Software

This section focuses on software products for authoring, presenting and publishing office documents, in the following referred to as office communication software. This market segment contains word processing, spreadsheet, presentation, database, and personal information management tools (Lufthansa 1998c). Generally, the different products of each supplier are integrated with each other, meaning that data can be exchanged between applications without compatibility problems. In contrast to this, the data exchange between applications of different suppliers usually leads to costs because of file incompatibility (Liebowitz/Margolis 1999, 141). Software suppliers usually also offer a bundle of the most common products, referred to as *office suites*, which are sold cheaper than the sum of the individual products.

In the following, the three major markets in the area of office communication (word processors, spreadsheets, and office suites) will be analyzed further, mainly focusing on the US market. The examination is based on empirical studies by Liebowitz and Margolis (1999) who use data sources from Dataquest (a division of GartnerGroup) and IDC (International Data Corporation). The results will be complemented by data from the study mentioned above and by a case study with the central information management unit at Lufthansa AG which shows how the use of office communication software is managed in large companies.

3.4.1 Spreadsheets

An overview of the spreadsheet market in 1982 shows about eighteen different products for various systems like Apple II, IBM PC, or Atari 800. The prices ranged from around $250 to $695. In 1983 Lotus entered the market with Lotus 1-2-3 ($495) which soon outperformed and outsold VisiCalc, the earliest spreadsheet software and until then the most successful one. VisiCalc finally disappeared in 1985 after the company was taken over by Lotus. At that time most spreadsheets were designed for IBM PCs due to the growing popularity of this system. Besides Lotus as the market leader, many other vendors existed in the market such as Computer Associates (Easy Planner, $195), Ashton-Tate (Framework, $695), Software Publishing (PFS Plan, $140), IBM (PlannerCalc, $80, and Multiplan 2.0, $195), Microsoft (Excel for Mac, $495, and Multiplan 2.0 for PC, $195).

After Microsoft introduced Excel for the PC (running under Windows) and Borland introduced Quattro for DOS in 1987, Microsoft, Borland, and Lotus soon dominated the market and competed for market share.

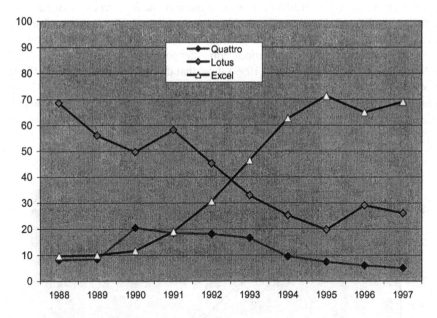

Figure 17: Shipments (units) share of spreadsheets (in %).

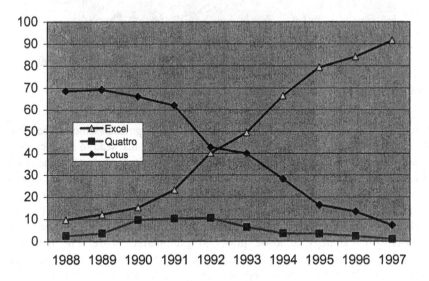

Figure 18: Revenue share of spreadsheets.

Figure 17 and Figure 18 show the success story of Microsoft which took over the market with around 90% revenue share in 1997. This evolution of the spreadsheet market seems be a contradiction to lock-in phenomena in markets with network effects. Traditional literature finds that it is very hard if not impossible for competitors to enter a market, which is already dominated by a certain product. Analyzing quality ratings from various computer journals over a ten years period (1988-1998) Liebowitz/Margolis (1999) show that despite existing network effects Lotus lost almost all of its market share because it had the inferior product. They observed significantly better ratings for Microsoft Excel since 1991 which corresponds with the revenue share chart where Microsoft had strong increases in 1991 and the following years.

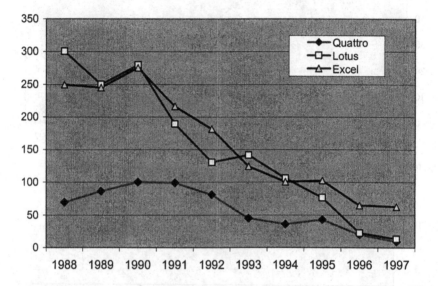

Figure 19: Spreadsheets prices (received by the vendor).

A look at the prices of spreadsheets confirms this hypothesis since it becomes obvious that it was not the pricing strategy of Microsoft that lead to the success of its software. While Borland stuck to an (unsuccessful) discount strategy, the prices of Lotus and Microsoft are rather similar and significantly decreasing over time. It also becomes clear that Lotus did not aggressively undercut Microsoft's prices until 1996 when Microsoft was already the dominant vendor. Of course it remains unclear whether Microsoft followed Lotus' price reductions or whether it was part of Microsoft's strategy to lower prices to gain market share. The failure of Borland's discount strategy also contradicts approaches which state that penetration pricing is the most effective strategy in network effect markets.

3.4.2 Word Processors

As in the market for spreadsheets, several competing word processing products existed in the 1980s. Figure 20 shows the most important applications, their revenue market shares. In 1986 the market shares of the six leading products were all below 20%. Although WordPerfect was the market leader it was closely followed by competitors like MultiMate and WordStar.

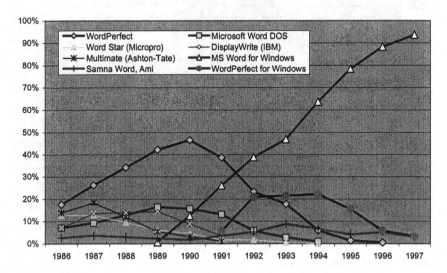

Figure 20: Word processor revenue market shares.

After 1986 WordPerfect constantly gained market share until it reached the peak of nearly 50% in 1990 leaving its competitors far behind. The figure illustrates the fact that with the growing popularity of Windows as an operating system, the market shares of DOS-based word processors declined until they finally completely disappeared. At the same time Microsoft Word for Windows, introduced in 1989, grew at an extraordinary rate until it reached over 90% of market share in 1997. WordPerfect for Windows, introduced about two years later than the Microsoft product, quickly gained about 20% of the market and remained at that level for a few years. Since 1995 (when WordPerfect for DOS was already meaningless) the share of WordPerfect for Windows decreased strongly and by 1997 it was already clear that this product was very likely to disappear from the market. AmiPro as an early competitor in the Windows market never reached significant market share in terms of actual revenue.

Liebowitz and Margolis (1999) again argue that it was the superior quality of Microsoft Word for Windows which, at a time where consumers were rethinking their decisions (because of the shift from DOS to Windows), led to the dominant position of this product. Looking at computer journal ratings Microsoft nearly always won the competition. The closest competitor in terms of quality was AmiPro which started with a much smaller installed base. While WordPerfect for DOS was once the leader in quality and market share, WordPerfect for Windows was late in the market and rated poorly, leading to its failure.

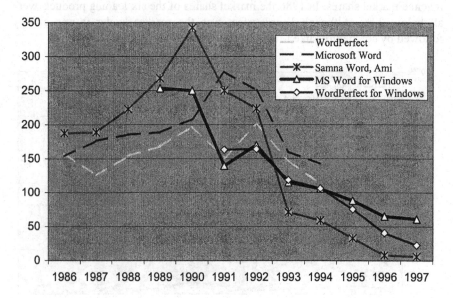

Figure 21: Word processor prices.

Looking at Figure 21, it becomes obvious that there is not much evidence that price strategies played a significant role in the failure of some products and the success of others. Very much like the market for spreadsheets the prices of the strongest competitors, WordPerfect for Windows and Microsoft Word for Windows, are very similar and have constantly decreased since 1992.

3.4.3   Office Suites

While in the early 1990s most of the products in the office software market were sold as stand-alone products, in recent years there has been a significant shift towards office suites (Figure 22).

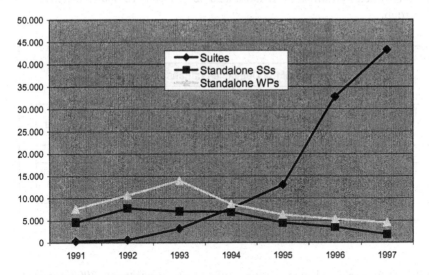

Figure 22: Number of suites and stand-alone software.

The relevance of office suites for today's software markets becomes clear when one looks at the fact that they account for about 50% of Microsoft's software market revenue (Liebowitz/Margolis 1999, 150). By 1997 products included in suites were practically not sold as stand-alone applications anymore. For example, suites already accounted for 95% of spreadsheets unit sales (Liebowitz/Margolis 1999, 146). As shown, Microsoft components generally got better ratings than the products of its competitors. In addition the early introduction of the MS office suite supporting all common user requirements fueled the great success of Microsoft. WordPerfect, Borland, and later Novell were slow in integrating their stand-alone products in to a sufficient suite.

3.4.4   Case Study: Standardization of Office Communication Software at Deutsche Lufthansa AG

With 55.000 employees, revenues of more than $13.4 billion, 43.8 million passengers, and 1.75 tons of freight in 1999, Deutsche Lufthansa AG is one of the largest air lines in the world. The group consists of more than 250 subsidiaries and associated companies which are either airline companies or belong to the tourist or airport ground handling businesses, such as logistics, maintenance, catering or IT service provider.

As far as IT standardization is concerned, rules and guidelines developed by the central MIS department (Konzern-Informationsmanagement, KIM) and passed by the IM-Board (see section 4.3.4.2) have become mandatory for all companies which are owned by Lufthansa by more than 50%. Figure 23 shows the structure of the group.

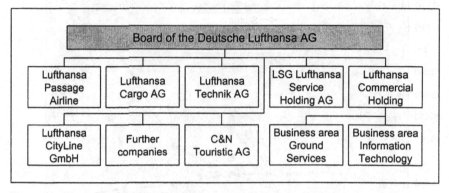

Figure 23: Companies of the Lufthansa Group.

In 1998 Lufthansa conducted a study called *Office-Konzeption 2000* aimed at developing standardization recommendations for client-side software applications in the back office area for the coming 18 months (Lufthansa Konzern-Informationsmanagement 1998c). The study resulted in recommendations which were passed as standardization rules by the IM board and came into effect after being published in December 1998.

Generally, one goal of the study was to modernize the back office software in terms of changes of user requirements and technological improvements in software products. Another goal was to standardize the IT-systems of Lufthansa group-wide as a means of lowering the Total Costs of Ownership (TCO) (Renn/Guptill 1998). Back office activities were distinguished in the three areas *communication*, *coordination*, and *cooperation*, which were examined separately by identifying the relevant technologies and standardization requirements (see Table 18). The technologies were analyzed by systematically using the following schema:

- description of the technology (modules, and areas of application)

- situation at Lufthansa (status quo and planned use of the respective technology)

- market analysis (status quo and future trends)

- analysis of alternatives (technologies, standards, and/or products as possible substitutes for the existing solution)

- evaluation

- standardization recommendations/rules

- migration plan

While the study covered all areas of standardization (illustrated by Table 18, in the remainder of this section, the focus will be on office communication software (referred to by Lufthansa as Office Productivity) consisting of software for authoring, presentation and publishing (Lufthansa Konzern-Informations-management 1998c, 76-84). Since there are many possible purchasing procedures (e.g. the independent companies of the Lufthansa Group can buy software independently or use the central purchasing department), it is hard to estimate the total spending on office communication software. The central MIS department estimates that today about 20,000 computers are equipped with NT and Microsoft Office software.

In 1998 the group-wide standard for office communication software was Microsoft Office 4.3 meaning that it was mandatory to use the relevant format whenever documents had to be exchanged. Nevertheless, some of the Lufthansa companies were already using MS Office 97 leading to transformation costs. The increasing market share of Office 97 also resulted in increasing costs for transforming external Office 97 documents to the (incompatible) Office 4.3 format. Additionally, the existing solution was seen as outdated as regards new requirements resulting from the increasing use of the Internet and the need for team cooperation. These reasons lead to the decision to modernize office communication software throughout the whole group within 18 months in terms of the following requirements:

- backward compatibility with Office 4.3 for document formats

- integration with the existing messaging solution (Microsoft Exchange) to improve team coordination

- support of publishing documents on the newly created Intranet

- user friendly solution in terms of low Total Costs of Ownership

The office suites of Corel (Office Professional), Lotus (SmartSuite), Microsoft (Microsoft Office), and the German vendor Star Division (Star Office 5.0) were evaluated. Microsoft was seen as the leading company in terms of technical quality and market share of the product. The market situation was influenced by the introduction of new releases of all vendors (an exception was Microsoft whose Office 2000 was announced for spring 1999).

Various new trends in the market were identified: The integration of the office suites with group ware systems of the relevant vendors allows the use of the software in a team context. New functions allow the direct publication of content on the World Wide Web without the need for additional tools. Proprietary formats seem to be complemented or replaced by Internet document formats like HTML or XML. There is a higher degree of integration in the area of user interfaces: a shift can be observed from a function-oriented to a document-oriented view, meaning that the functionality (word processing, spreadsheets) is offered when needed in a certain context. Although the potential benefits in an office communication environment are not yet clear, many vendors offer voice recognition tools. To fulfill the increasing need to individualize office software there is a trend towards "modularizing" standard software solutions and additionally offering development tools.

After the general analysis of the status quo at Lufthansa and the market, the alternatives were evaluated by comparing various attributes of the products. Table 14 gives an overview of the evaluation. It presents all the information the decision was based on.

Table 14: Decision criteria for office software.

	Office 97	Office 2000 (beta 1)	SmartSuite Millenium	StarOffice 5.0	Office Professional
General					
Vendor	Microsoft	Microsoft	Lotus	Star Division	Corel
Price	$599	?	$472	$128	$445
Platform	Win95, Win98, NT	Win95, Win98, NT	Win95, Win98, NT, Win 3.1, OS/2	Win95, Win98, NT, Linux, OS/2	Win95, Win NT 4.0
Backward compatibility					
Format	Converter	Converter	Converter	Converter	Converter
Macros	no	no	no	no	no
Internet integration					
HTML as data format	yes	yes	yes	yes	yes
Web-server publishing	no	yes (FTP or proprietary tools)	yes (FTP, Domino)	yes	no
Other	-	XML and CSS support	XML support, compatible with eSuite applets	HTML-editor, XML support	Barista-technology (Java-viewer)

Table 14: (continued)

Functionality					
Word processor	Word	Word	WordPro	StarWriter	WordPerfect 7
Spreadsheet	Excel	Excel	1-2-3	StarCalc	Quattro Pro 7
Database	Access8	Access8 / UNICODE	Approach	StarBase	Paradox 7
Presenta-tion	PowerPoint	PowerPoint	Freelance	StarImpress	Presentations
Personal Information Manage-ment (PIM)	Outlook	Outlook	Organizer	none	InfoCentral
Drawing	none	none	none	StarDraw	CorelDraw 9
Voice recognition	none	none	IBM ViaVoice	none	IBM ViaVoice
Web browser	none	Internet Explorer 5.0	none	none	Netscape Navigator 2.0
Other	-	-	Screen Cam-Screen Capture, FastSite Web-publishing, SmartCenter	StarSche-dule, StarMail, StarDiscuss	CorelFLOW, SideKick, Envoy
Team work support					
Integration with Exchange	yes	yes	no	no information	no information
Other	-	Discussions, comments, Web subscription	integration with Lotus Domino	Web subscription	-

Table 14: (continued)

User friendliness				
Help function	yes	yes	yes	yes	yes
Assistants	yes	yes	no	no	yes
Other	-	dynamic interface adaption		Autopilot (automated processes)	-
Installation and migration				
Install on-demand	no	yes	no	no information	no
Administered installation	yes	yes	with Tivoli	no information	yes
Self-repair	no	yes	no	no information	no
Other	-	2 versions of MS Office can simultaneous ly be run	-	only vendor with platform independent solution	-

After evaluating the alternatives based on the relevant criteria, the following recommendation was given by the Lufthansa central MIS department (this recommendation was passed by the IM-board at the end of 1998 and came into effect on 1 January 1999): To reduce the TCO, Microsoft Office 97 was defined as the future document exchange format. Since the new release was expected shortly, Lufthansa companies also were allowed to use MS Office 2000. If possible the migration to Office 97 was be combined with an upgrade to Windows NT. During the migration period of 6 months compatibility was to be guaranteed by using the respective tools, e.g. to transform Office 4.3 into Office 97 files. 1 July 1999 was set as the end of the migration period. This meant that prior to this critical date the early adopters had to avoid incompatibilities by transforming their files back to Office 4.3 format whenever they had to exchange documents. After this date the late adopters had to bear the costs of incompatibilities by transforming their files to Office 97 format before exchanging them.

3.5 Comparison of Different Software Markets

This section will summarize the empirical analysis of the different software markets and compare the results. The specific differences in the markets have to be taken into account when buying decisions and diffusion processes are modeled (see section 6).

To evaluate relevant decision criteria like functionality, price, and various types of direct and indirect network effects for the different software categories, the MIS managers of the 1000 largest companies in Germany and the US were asked to evaluate the influence of network effects on their decisions on software. The respondents evaluated selected criteria by choosing from a five-category scale with the extremes "very important and "unimportant".

Current and future market penetration was used as an indicator of direct network effects in terms of the installed base. In contrast to this, the relevance of direct network effects within their own business network was evaluated by asking whether it was important that the particular solution is widely used among their business partners. Criteria for indirect network effects were the importance of consulting services and other complementary goods as well as the experience of employees with the software. Figure 24 illustrates the results for the different software categories. Note that for reasons of simplification the figure does not include the fifth category ("unimportant") since none of the profile plots was in this category. The results can be summarized as follows.

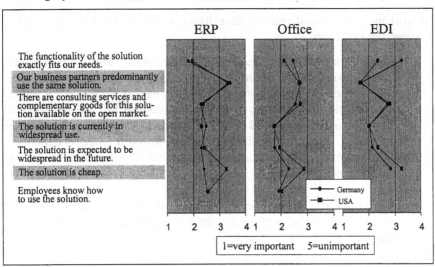

Figure 24: How important are selected factors for decisions on software?

Firstly, it is obvious that the profiles in Germany and the United States are very similar. Exceptions are the importance of EDI functionality, which is rated less important by the German respondents, and the evaluation of software costs (where MIS managers from the US seem to be less sensitive than their German colleagues). The latter might result from the fact that the responding US companies are generally much larger in size, leading to higher discounts (Office Software) or efficiency advantages through higher data volume (ERP, EDI).

As expected, direct and indirect network effects are an important criterion for the decision on software. More interesting is the fact that the profiles vary significantly between software categories. It is obvious that the relevance of network effects and functionality is different for ERP systems, office software and EDI solutions. For example, direct network effects through communication with business partners are less important for ERP software, which is commonly used to organize internal processes than for office software or even more significantly for EDI solutions. Besides this, there is another astonishing result which will be important in the further analysis: the direct network effects within a category vary depending on whether adopters within the individual network of business partners or within the entire market network (installed base) are taken into account. While the current and expected adoption in the market is rated similarly for all categories, the importance of adoption among business partners differs significantly. In contrast to many existing models of network effects which consider only the whole installed base (see section 4), in the software market the individual communication network environment seems to play an especially important role. This hypothesis will later be substantiated by simulations modeling the software market as a relational diffusion network (section 6).

Summarizing the empirical analysis, the software market for **ERP systems** can be characterized as follows.

- *Market structure:* The supplier side of the market in the US is rather heterogeneous with stable user clusters of the competing products with similar market share. In contrast to this, the market in Germany is rather monopolistic, dominated by SAP with the products R/2 and R/3. Due to the high costs, the demand side of the market consists mainly of large companies. Currently, suppliers are also tring to win SMEs as customers by modularizing their solutions and by creating downsized and therefore cheaper products.

- *Price segment:* Cost overviews show that this market is part of the high price segment. German MIS managers are more price sensitive in this area than their colleagues from the US.

- *The role of network effects and compatibility:* Compared with other software, MIS managers see business software as the area with the most significant problems of incompatibility within the company (see Figure 35). Therefore, standardized ERP systems are strategically used to integrate the subsidiaries of large groups. Since the benefits of standardization occur at the level of the whole company instead of single subsidiaries or departments, this decision is made centrally or at least the central MIS participates in the decision process (see also Table 19). While compatibility within ones own subsidiaries or departments is the main reason for choosing standardized products, it is generally of low relevance whether business partners use the same solution (Figure 24). In contrast to this, the current and future installed base in the whole market is of high importance, similar to the availability of complementary goods like consulting services in the market. Nevertheless, focusing on the individual situation of single companies, the case of Heraeus shows that there can be standardization pressure from important business partners towards implementing an ERP system and the choice of the product.

- *Preferences towards functionality:* In comparison with other criteria, the functionality of the solution in terms of supporting the company-specific business processes is of greatest importance. The preferences towards ERP systems are heterogeneous, since every individual company has its own individual requirements. Even typical business processes for certain industries are not yet covered by the standard software products (e.g. the case of Fachverlag). This leads to costly customizing and a large proportion of custom-made modules (inhouse-made), respectively. Nevertheless, the empirical study shows a clear trend in this context: About 82% of the MIS managers in Germany who responded and 90% in the US agree (or totally agree) that their companies will use more standardized business software in the future. At the same time a majority of the respondents (77.2% in Germany and 71.4% in the US) believes that standard software will be easier to customize.

The software market for **EDI solutions** can be characterized as follows.

- *Market structure:* There are many suppliers of EDI solutions, often specialized in certain industries or EDI standards respectively, since the systems are complex and the standards differ significantly. While many (mostly incompatible) different EDI standards exist in the German market, this heterogeneity was not found in the USA. Up to now EDI solutions were mostly used by large companies, which could more easily over-compensate for the high costs by cost savings due to the large amounts of data exchanged with business partners. In the near future, standardized, more flexible, and cheaper Internet-based solutions will also allow SMEs to use EDI products.

- *Price segment:* The market belongs to the high price segment with a high proportion of custom-made solutions. With the emergence of WebEDI this is likely to change. The market is moving to standardized products in the lower price segment.

- *The role of network effects and compatibility:* In contrast to ERP systems, in the context of EDI, compatibility with external business partners is at the center of attention. Therefore, the most important decision criterion by far is that communication partners within ones own business network use the same solution. By contrast, functionality, the existence of complementary goods, and price are of relatively low importance. Network effects formerly deriving from the relevant EDI-standard alone will derive from product-related (supplier) standards in the future. This will change the dynamics of this market drastically. New suppliers like Commerce One Inc., Ariba Inc., etc. enter the market with their Internet-related knowledge with marketing strategies (especially price and product policy) that consider product-related network effect.

- *Preferences towards functionality:* In the past, EDI solutions were based on the relevant EDI-standard. Besides restrictions of the standard itself, the functionality of an EDI solution was determined by the quality of custom-made programming aimed at mapping the in-house data structure to the structure of the EDI standard. Since the requirements of the data structure differ strongly between industries and companies, the preference for a certain EDI standard was most important. As described above, this is likely to change. Preferences will shift from certain EDI standards to standardized products with flexible data mapping and various data formats.

The market for **office communication software** can be characterized as follows.

- *Market structure:* The market for office communication software is a good example of an evolution towards high market concentration. While there were many competing suppliers in the 80ies, the market is now completely dominated by Microsoft. This monopolistic structure lead to the Antitrust litigation which is broadly and controversially discussed in the literature (e.g. Katz/Shapiro 1998, Liebowitz/Margolis 1999). The demand side of the market is characterized by a large number of potential buyers, ranging from large corporation to individuals.

- *Price segment:* Office communication software clearly belongs to the low price segment. The prices have strongly decreased over time (see Figure 25). The low price reduces the lock in to a certain solution meaning that it is easier for a consumer to switch to another (superior) product. In contrast to ERP systems or EDI solutions, many users have changed their office communication products within recent years (e.g. Liebowitz/Margolis 1999, 141-143).

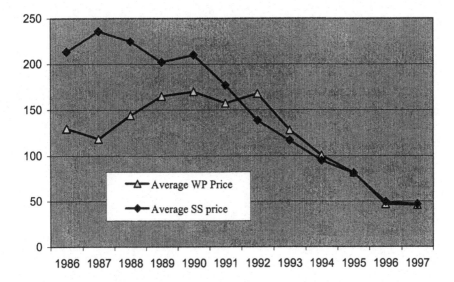

Figure 25: Average prices for spreadsheets (SS) and word processor (WP) in the PC, or IBM-compatible market.

- *The role of network effects and compatibility:* Compatibility with business partners is relevant, but not as important as the current and future installed base (also knowledge of employees) of the whole market. Nevertheless, the case study of Lufthansa shows that compatibility within the individual communication network also plays an important role when deciding about office communication software. This is the reason why the central MIS puts great effort in unifying solutions in the individual independent Lufthansa companies.

- *Preferences for functionality:* The market for office communication software is a market with relatively homogenous preferences (i.e. all users have similar needs in terms of spreadsheet software, word processors, etc.). The Lufthansa study *Office-Konzeption 2000* shows that different products can be compared and evaluated using a certain set of software attributes. Confirming the hypothesis of homogenous preferences, Liebowitz/Margolis (1999) demonstrate that in this market, despite possibly strong network effects, the product with the highest quality will outsell the competition and finally dominate the market.

4 Modeling Decisions on Software Standards in Information Networks

After empirically studying various software markets, it will now be analyzed whether existing approaches are sufficient to deal with their dynamics and heterogeneous properties. This section will focus on so-called standardization models aimed at describing and solving the decision problem concerning the selection of the right communication standards to support data exchange in information networks.

The empirical analysis of section 3 revealed two typical decision situations when the focus is on the corporate use of software products for data exchange.

On the one hand, from the perspective of a central coordinating unit (such as the MIS department of Lufthansa) standardization rules might be set to optimize data exchange within a company or a group of companies. In terms of the costs and benefits of competing software solutions for all units simultaneously, the decision problem arises, which unit (individual, department, company, etc.) of the organization should use which software product at what time. Generally, this is referred to as the *centralized standardization problem*.

On the other hand, whenever there is no central coordinating unit in information networks (good examples are business networks with independent companies or the Internet) the decisions on software for data exchange are still interdependent due to the need of compatibility. The problem of coordinating the use of software in such decentralized networks in generally referred to as the *decentralized standardization problem*.

In the following, the existing approaches of Buxmann, König, and Weitzel for both scenarios will be described (e.g. Buxmann 1996, Buxmann/König 1998, Buxmann/Weitzel/König 1999). To examine the possibility of extensions it will further be analyzed how the idea of intermediaries might be integrated into these models, since the market also offers the outsourcing of compatibility problems (in the context of data exchange) by using intermediaries specialized in data format transformation. The relevance of such institutions was demonstrated in the empirical study and can be seen, for example, for the area of EDI in Table 1. The models will then be evaluated on a general level by using empirical data from the study described above. It will then be analyzed whether the approaches are helpful in modeling the buying decisions in software markets and whether they are capable of describing the dynamic and variety of real world diffusion courses.

4.1 Centralized Decisions on Communication Standards in Information Networks

Buxmann 1996 models the centralized standardization problem by describing information networks as directed graphs. The nodes represent the participants of the network and the edges their communication relationships. The basic idea is that the use of the same communication standard facilitates the exchange of information between the respective nodes resulting in cost reductions. Using a standard results in *standardization costs*, e.g. costs for buying a certain product and for implementing and running the solution.

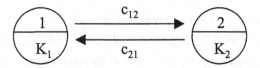

Figure 26: Standardization costs and benefits (Buxmann/Weitzel/König 1999).

Figure 26 shows the standardization costs and benefits. If node 1 and node 2 implement a certain standard they have to pay the standardization costs K_1 and K_2, respectively. If both nodes use the same standard (and only then) they save communication costs c_{12} and c_{21}. In a centrally coordinated network like the Lufthansa Group, the coordinating unit faces the problem of deciding which standards to implement in the various nodes at what time. It has to simultaneously consider the trade-off between standardization costs and benefits for all nodes.

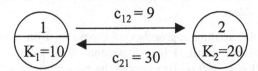

Figure 27: Coordination problem with 2 nodes (Buxmann/Weitzel/König 1999).

Figure 27 shows an exemplary coordination problem with two nodes. It is obvious that it is advantageous to standardize for both nodes (from a central perspective).

The standardization surplus is (9+30) – (10+20) = 9 monetary units. From the individual perspective of the two nodes the standardization is only profitable for node 2. Since the focus of the centralized model is on the optimization of the network as a whole, it does not matter whether costs and benefits for individual nodes are positive or not. Based on linear programming, the authors introduce a method of solving the standardization problem in networks. A binary indicative variable x_j takes on the value 1 if a particular standard is used by node j (resulting in costs of K_j) and 0 if not. Therefore, the standardization costs of the whole network add up to $\sum_{i=1}^{n} K_i x_i$. Modeling the cost savings, the binary variable y_{ij} is introduced, taking on the value 0 whenever two connected nodes i and j use the same standard. The target function for optimizing the standardization decisions for the whole network can than be described as follows:

$$\sum_{i=1}^{n} K_i x_i + \sum_{i=1}^{n} \sum_{\substack{j=1 \\ j \neq i}}^{n} c_{ij} y_{ij} \rightarrow Min!$$

The model calculates the optimal allocation of standards to all nodes in given communications networks. While the model described above covers the case of a single standard and a single period, other scenarios might also be considered by adjusting the model.

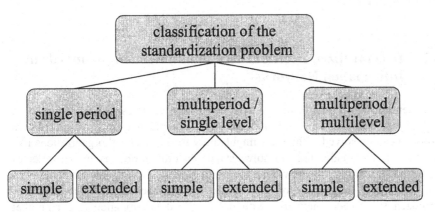

Figure 28: Dimensions of the standardization problem.

Figure 28 shows how the standardization problem can be differentiated into the various dimensions (Buxmann 1996, Buxmann/Weitzel/Westarp/König 1999). The single period standardization problem assumes that all advantages and disadvantages of the standardization that occur are unrelated to time. In turn, the multiperiod and single level standardization problem implies that the advantages and disadvantages of standardization can occur at different points in time, for which the resulting payments are to be discounted to the time the decision was made. The decision to use standards, however, is only made once at the beginning of the planning horizon - similar to a simple investment-theoretical approach. The multiperiod and multilevel standardization problem also allows decisions to be made during different periods of the planning horizon. Each of these dimensions can be further differentiated into a simple and an extended standardization problem. The simple problem assumes only one standard is available, while the extended problem also includes the decision to choose one standard from a selection of available alternative standards.

Buxmann/Weitzel/König (1999) identify various problems concerning the real world application of the model resulting in coordination costs for the central unit. A *data problem* occurs since real world network participants behave opportunistically. It might be advantageous for individual nodes to hide their real standardization costs and benefits from the central unit in order to avoid possible disadvantages, e.g. if the individual standardization costs of the node are higher than the benefits. A *complexity problem* occurs since the model describes an np-complete problem in the case of multiple standards which is extremely difficult to solve, especially with increasing network sizes, a set of multiple standards, and if more than one period is considered. In the real world an *implementation problem* also occurs. Calculating the first-best solution for a communication network does not mean that participants will consider the result when choosing their solutions. Even in hierarchical organizations the control and incentive system results in coordination costs.

4.2   Decentralized Decisions on Communication Standards in Information Networks

The centralized standardization model implicitly assumes the existence of a central coordinating unit and that the data, complexity, and implementation problem can be solved. While this might apply for hierarchical organizations like companies, the model fails to solve standardization problems in networks of independent actors with individual costs and benefits. Taking the restrictions of the centralized standardization model into account the authors extended their approach to consider networks with decentralized coordination (meaning that participants independently decide on the use of standards) (Buxmann/Weitzel/König 1999). Each node is modeled with its own decision power, namely whether to implement a certain standard or not. The nodes have to bear their standardization costs and benefit from standardization whenever a communication partner uses the same communication standard. In contrast to the centralized model where the central unit had complete information about costs and benefits, the information of the nodes in the decentralized model is restricted. It is assumed that participants in the network know the standardization costs of all other nodes. The nodes also know their own potential savings which they might be able to realize when using the same standard as well as the savings of the relevant communication partner. The potential savings between other nodes are not known. The idea of the model is that every node bases its decision on a prediction of the standardization decision of its communication partners. The expected utility for implementing a particular standard is described by the following function:

$$E\,[U(i)] = \sum_{\substack{j=1 \\ j \neq i}}^{n} p_{ij}\, c_{ij} - K_i$$

In this term the p_{ij} is the probability reflecting how much participant i believes that its respective communication partners will implement the same standard. Participant i will implement the standard whenever the expected utility is positive. Based on the restricted knowledge of each participant the authors calculate p_{ij} as follows. A participant i knows the potential savings c_{ji} of its communication partner j when both use the same standard. The assumption that c_{ij} is representative for all other edges of j leads to the following estimation of p_{ij}:

$$p_{ij} = \frac{c_{ji}(n-1) - K_j}{c_{ji}(n-1)}$$

The numerator describes the possible standardization surplus (savings minus costs) for node j when all its communication partners also standardize (best-case). The denominator normalizes the term to a value between 0 and 1. With increasing savings compared to the costs, the probability increases that j implements the standard. If j has only advantages and no costs through standardization, p_{ij} becomes 1 meaning that node i can be sure that j will implement the standard. Whenever the term $c_{ji}(n-1) - K_j$ is negative then $p_{ij} = 0$ holds since node j will not standardize when the costs are greater than the benefits. In contrast to the centralized standardization model which calculates the first-best solution for a given network, the decentralized model is not aiming at solving the standardization problem but at analyzing standardization behavior under more realistic assumptions. Buxmann/Weitzel/König (1999) conducted simulations to compare standardization processes in centralized and decentralized networks in terms of efficiency. For reasons of simplification, the one standard problem was examined, meaning that participants could either implement a certain standard or not. A network of 20 nodes was used with the standardization costs K_i being normally distributed with μ=10,000 and σ=1,000 and the edge-related savings c_{ij} being normally distributed with σ=200. The expected value μ of the savings was continuously increased in a range from 0 to 1,700. 100 runs were conducted for each parameter constellation. Figure 29 shows the results. Note that the edge-related savings are referred to as information costs by the authors who actually mean the *reduction of information costs* by standardization.

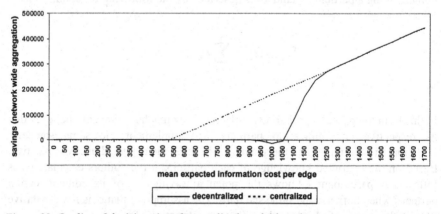

Figure 29: Quality of decisions in a decentralized model based upon ex post network-wide savings on information costs for alternative $E[c_{ij}]$ (Buxmann/Weitzel/König 1999).

The figure shows the following results for the given example: For expected savings between 0 and 530, none of the nodes standardize in either network since the negative difference between costs and benefits is too high. In the area of 1,282 and above, both networks completely standardize meaning that everybody implements the standard since the positive difference between costs and benefits is significant enough. For expected values between 531 and 1,281 there is a *standardization gap* meaning that in networks which use the decentralized mechanism fewer participants than the optimum (or the wrong participants) implement the standard.

4.3 The Role of Intermediaries

Evaluating whether the standardization models are suitable for software markets, it has to be examined if they are flexible enough to be capable of considering the typical characteristics of such markets. Using the example of intermediation in communication networks (see Table 1), this section will show what potential extensions might look like. As described above, participants in information networks face the decision problem of choosing the appropriate set of software standards for their bilateral communication links. The existence of intermediaries in software markets specialized in data format transformation offers yet another alternative. The question arises whether or not it is more efficient to support the standards of the communication partners, or whether the compatibility problem should be outsourced to an intermediary. In the following, the possible efficiency increases resulting from the use of such intermediary services are analyzed. On the basis of the centralized standardization model, a model is introduced which describes the decision problem and solves it for a centrally coordinated network. The idea is that an actor who implements multiple software standards can also offer transformation services, thereby reducing its own costs. Like the approach described above, the model is based on linear programming. For a given information network, it determines the optimum set of software standards for each participant, and the optimum number of intermediaries, as well as their optimum service range.

4.3.1 Efficiency Increases Through Intermediaries in Information Networks

Many software products which are used for professional data exchange within business networks are characterized by relatively high set-up costs, together with lower variable costs of data transmission (e.g. Emmelhainz 1993). Experience shows that a critical limit exists with regard to the amount of data, after which the solution is economically viable. Due to the high dynamics of the software market and the short life-cycle of products, the set-up costs must be relatively quickly compensated for by variable cost savings. Therefore, especially for smaller companies with small amounts of data, the problem is whether or not such a change is worthwhile. Transaction costs can present a further barrier. These can result from companies' concerns about losing their independence or existing business connections. In the past, for example, the automotive industry showed how market-dominating manufacturers forced their own EDI standard onto their suppliers. In complex information networks such as the automotive sector, this leads to a problem referred to as the *insider-outsider problem*. Supposing a supplier joins the communication standard of one of its customers, it automatically becomes more difficult to support the already existing communication links to their other customers and suppliers. The reason is that sustaining the technology of old standards continues to incur costs dependent on the amount of data. However, these are then allocated to a smaller amount of data. As an example, one can imagine what it means to continue keeping up the telex standard for communicating with some partners. In addition, as with all standards, the uncertainty still remains if, and to what extent, the software standard will prevail in the business world.

One issue of data services is to uncouple both the transmitter and the receiver in terms of time and technical aspects. For direct data exchange between two business partners, the transmitter's computer system reaches the receiver's system, for example, by using a telephone line. Both systems must be compatible. This refers to technical attributes on the one hand, such as the transmission speed determined by the communications protocol. On the other hand, organizational attributes, such as the system's operating time, must be synchronized for data transmission. Suppose a manufacturer has several customers, possibly using different computer or communication systems, maybe even located in different time zones, then the result is a complex, costly system of direct point-to-point connections.

Assuming an intermediary takes over basic responsibilities, such as receiving, storing, and forwarding electronic data, then many of the connections necessary for direct communication can be eliminated. In a formal approach, this relation can be derived from the law of contact cost reduction (Balderston 1958, Baligh/Richartz 1967). An information network with n participants, each sustaining communication links to every other participant, results to $n(n-1)/2$ communication links. By employing an intermediary, the number can be reduced to n. Figure 30 illustrates the connection.

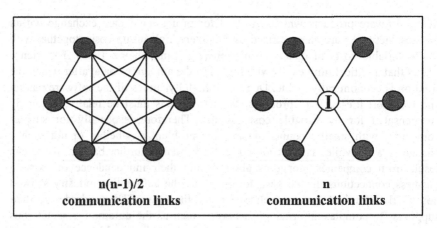

$$n(n-1)/2$$
communication links

n
communication links

Figure 30: Contact reduction.

For n>3 a reduction of edges results for the whole communication system, independent of the amount of data to be transmitted; the number of communication contacts decreases correspondingly. The problems of synchronization in terms of time and technical compatibility are reduced. However, the intermediary must be capable of supporting the technical and organizational conditions of each participant in order to coordinate the reception and forwarding of data.

Other services offered by intermediaries in information networks are connected to data security. In exchanging business data, EDI users or users of other communication standards are often concerned with the security of sensitive data. In addition to authenticity, integrity, and confidentiality (Europäische Kommission 1997), a significant issue is system security. An intermediary specialized in forwarding data generally has more solid know-how in the area of data security than individual users, and furthermore has improved technical capabilities for taking any necessary security measures.

Next to services in the technical area, intermediaries in communication networks are primarily concerned with transforming content attributes of data. Two forms can be differentiated. *Format transformation* consists of the intermediary translating incoming electronic data with company-specifically formatted contents into the format of a business partner et vice versa. This reduces the insider-outsider effect. In cases where the transmitter and the receiver are using completely different storage or transferring mediums, an intermediary additionally conducts a *medium transformation*. Syntactic, semantic and pragmatic elements are determined and applied to the structure of the new medium. The presence of both technical and content attributes becomes clear, since the storage medium is also used for the physical data transfer. Medium transformation enables, for example, EDI data to be forwarded to the relevant receiver by mail, fax, e-mail, or telephone. An example for a supplier of such services is the Deutsche Post AG. The opposite case is much costlier, but also possible.

In addition to the potential efficiency increases mentioned above, intermediaries in information networks can realize economies of scope as well as economies of scale. The latter are especially attainable by grouping data while processing different services. Examples are clustering advantages for storage or transfer capacities or transferring grouped data during times of low network rates. In such a competitive market, the savings are passed on to the customer through lower prices.

By determining his service range, an intermediary decides for which communication standards and for which storage mediums he wishes to transform data into which EDI standards. All of these standards must be supported in his own organization and, additionally, he must have the appropriate transformation instruments available. The choice of service range depends on the consumers, whose needs the intermediary aims at satisfying.

4.3.2 Optimum Number of Intermediaries in Information Networks and Their Optimum Service Range

This section will introduce a model which optimizes the use of software standards in a centrally coordinated information network. As in the models described above, an information network is formally described as nodes connected by edges. Standardization costs are assigned to the nodes; the potential bilateral costs savings are assigned to the edges. Each node can perform intermediary functions if it is equipped with the standards to be transformed. In the business world, this assumption is confirmed by companies using company-internal know-how to supply data transfer services on the market. An example is debis, which, in addition to handling the data communication of its parent corporation Daimler Benz, supplies the service externally. If data is not directly transferred from a transmitting node to a receiving node, i.e. if an intermediary is used, a series of edges is passed through. For the transformation of data from one standard into another, variable transaction costs are incurred for the node conducting intermediary functions. These are the charges to the respective intermediary, dependent on the amount of data transferred. In the United States, for example, these costs range between \$0.20 and \$0.75 per 1,000 characters (Emmelhainz 1993, 112-117). Implementing a standard in a node is only worthwhile if the sum of variable cost savings outweighs the set-up costs. The costs of a company-internal implementation are weighed against the intermediary costs, i.e. the costs of having data transformed into the specific standard. A third alternative is, of course, maintaining the status quo of a node. Since coordinating standardization activities centrally seeks an optimum solution for the entire network, all possible constellations of standardization decisions of each participant must be compared. This shows that positive network effects are considered, since every possible constellation of such effects is implicitly enumerated in the solution process and therefore included in the comparison of alternatives.

The model optimizes an existing information network, consisting of n nodes with S available standards to choose from. The participants are already equipped with a certain software standard. When a node i ($i \in \{1,...,n\}$) is equipped with a standard s ($s \in \{0,...,S-1\}$), costs of $stancosts_{is}$ are incurred. The amount of information transferred in the communication link between nodes k and l ($k,l \in \{1,...,n\}$) is indicated by $flow_{kl}$. A flow along the edge between nodes i and j ($j \in \{1,...,n\}$) incurs variable costs of $comcosts_{ijs}$, dependent on the standard s being used. If an information flow transmitted in node i is transformed from standard s into standard t (or vice versa), variable costs of $trancosts_{ist}$ result. Nodes and edges are not subject to any capacity restrictions, i.e. no quantitative restrictions apply for redirecting or transforming data flows.

The action variables of the model are, on the one hand, the binary variable $X_{is} \in \{0,1\}$, assuming the value 1 if node i is equipped with standard s. On the other hand, the variable $F_{ijkls} \in R_{0+}$ (with $i \neq j$ and $k < l$), indicates the data flow transmitted from node k as the sender to node l as the receiver (subsequently referred to as „communication link (k,l)"), passing through edge (i,j) on its way to the target node.

The binary variable $Y_{ijkls} \in \{0,1\}$ (with $i < j$ and $k < l$) serves as an auxiliary variable of the model. It indicates whether a flow takes place along edge (i,j) using standard s for the communication link (k,l). Another auxiliary variable, $T_{iklst} \in \{0,1\}$ (with $k < l$ and $s < t$), indicates whether in node i a flow of the communication link (k,l) is transformed from standard s into standard t (or vice versa).

The model is static, i.e. fixed costs must be compensated for by potential variable cost savings within a specified service lifetime of the standard considered. This assumption is based on the dynamics already mentioned in connection with the development of new products, which make long-term planning unrealistic. The (first-best) cost optimum is determined from the overall viewpoint of the network.

The following target function determines the solution of the coordination problem for centrally coordinated networks:

$$costs =$$

$$\sum_{\substack{i,j,k,l,s \\ i<j \\ k<l}} comcosts_{ijs} \cdot (F_{ijkls} + F_{jikls}) + \sum_{i,s} stancosts_{is} \cdot X_{is}$$

$$+ \sum_{\substack{i,k,l,s,t \\ k<l \\ s<t}} flow_{kl} \cdot trancosts_{ist} \cdot T_{iklst}$$

$$\rightarrow min!$$

The constraints of the linear problem are illustrated in Westarp/Weber/Buxmann/König (1997). The solution resulting from the optimization can be used to determine the optimum total costs of the information network, the use of communication standards in each node, as well as the standards and the series of edges of each data transfer. In addition, the nodes functioning as intermediaries, the extent of data transformation, as well as the intermediary's range of standards can be determined. The following section illustrates an example of optimizing a given network.

4.3.3 Example of Optimizing an Information Network

In the following, an example of a network is optimized to illustrate the scope of the model. Figure 31 depicts an information network in its initial state.

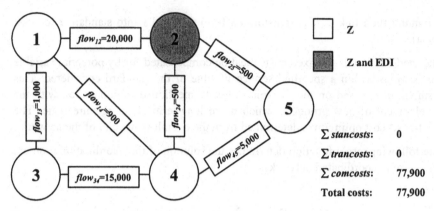

Figure 31: Initial state of the network.

To simplify, a network with only five participants is chosen, represented by nodes 1 through 5. Determined data flows take place along the communication links between the participants. The amount of data determined is listed along the edges. For example, 900 data units are exchanged between participant 1 and participant 4. In the initial state of the network each node is equipped with a software standard Z. Node 2 is additionally equipped with an EDI solution, symbolized by the shaded area in Figure 31. Communication within the entire network is based on the standard Z, since node 2 does not have a partner to communicate with using EDI. Variable costs are incurred along the edges for exchanging information. lists the amounts for both standards.

Table 15: Variable edge-related figures.

edge	(1,2)	(1,3)	(1,4)	(2,4)	(2,5)	(3,4)	(4,5)
volume of data	20,000	1,000	900	500	500	15,000	5,000
var. comcosts (Z)	1	1	1	1	1	3	2
var. comcosts (EDI)	0.5	0.5	0.5	0.5	0.5	1.5	1

The exchange of information between nodes 3 and 4, for example, incurs costs of 15,000*3=45,000 monetary units. The costs of the initial state therefore total 77,900 monetary units for the data exchange. At the same time, these costs represent the total costs of the information network, since no costs are incurred for implementing a new standard.

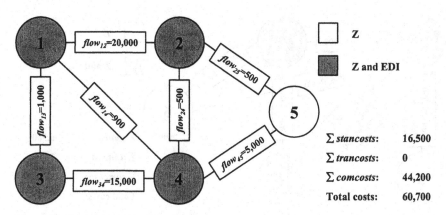

Figure 32: Optimum without intermediation.

Figure 32 presents the optimum standardization solution of the network without intermediaries. Based on the situation described above, it was evaluated whether it is economically viable to implement EDI in the individual nodes. Table 16 lists the respective standardization costs incurred.

Table 16: Node-related costs.

node	1	2	3	4	5
stancosts (EDI)	5,000	0	10,000	1,500	6,000
var. *trancosts*	0.1	1	0.25	0.2	0.2

The standardization costs of node 2 of course equal zero, since EDI is already available. Nodes 1 through 4 are equipped with EDI in the optimum, and use this standard to communicate. Standardization costs totaling 16,500 monetary units result. Node 5, on the other hand, continues to communicate with its partners using standard Z. The costs of transferring data amount to 44,200 monetary units, and therefore total costs of 60,700 monetary units result.

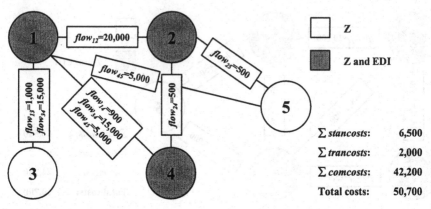

Figure 33: Optimum with intermediation.

Figure 33 shows the optimum solution for the network under consideration of intermediation. Considering the initial state, each node can take over intermediary functions. Table 16 lists the edge-specific variable costs incurred for transforming data.

In the optimum solution for this example, fewer nodes implement the EDI solution than in the solution without an intermediary. Only nodes 1 and 4 are additionally equipped with EDI. Node 1 serves as the intermediary. It directs data flows between nodes 3 and 4 and nodes 4 and 5. Along edge (1,4), for example, flow34=15,000 data units results, that is assigned to the communication link between nodes 3 and 4. The intermediary's service consists of transforming data from standard Z into the EDI standard, and vice versa. The participating nodes are charged a total of (15,000+5,000)*0.1=2,000 monetary units in transformation costs. It is clear that in this example, even with redirecting data, lower total costs result for the entire information network.

4.3.4 Empirical Evaluation of the Standardization Models

The evaluation of the standardization models will be carried out in four areas. First, the relevance of the standardization problem will generally be evaluated by empirically analyzing how heterogeneous software solutions in enterprises currently are, and to what extent compatibility problems arise. Then the Lufthansa case studies will show how the management of large enterprises deals with standardization problems by setting standardization and migration rules to support the process of unifying software solutions. In a third step, the parameters of the models will be evaluated. Finally, the question of centralization vs. decentralization of decisions in companies will be addressed. The section ends with a summary of the results.

4.3.4.1   Heterogeneity and Compatibility Problems

To gain information about the heterogeneity of software solutions in companies the respondents were asked about the number of different products they have currently in use in the different categories. Figure 34 illustrates what percentage of the responding companies uses how many products in each of the listed software categories. The upper and lower bars of each category show the results in Germany and in the US respectively.

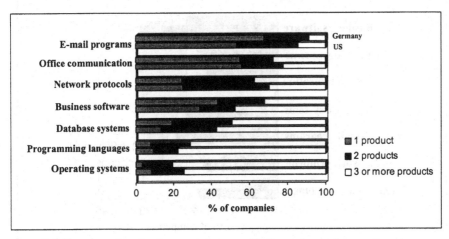

Figure 34: Heterogeneity of software products used in the various software categories.

Comparing the two countries, the results do not reveal a significant difference in terms of the variety of products. *Business software* is an exception to this. More than 68% of the German companies who responded only use one or two products in this category, while it is only 53% of the companies in the US. This remarkable gap of 15% is most probably a result of the dominant market position of SAP software in Germany. The largest variety of standards is found in the area of *programming languages* and *operating systems*. Only 29% of the largest companies in Germany use fewer than three programming languages (23% in the US) and only 20% (26% in the US) use fewer than three operating systems. In contrast, less variety is found in the categories *e-mail programs* and *office communication*. About 92% of the responding German companies (86% in US) use only one or two different products for their e-mail communication and 73% (78% in US) use only one or two different office communication products.

Looking at the variety of products in use does not necessarily provide enough information about related incompatibility problems. Therefore, the respondents were asked to give their evaluation of the incompatibility problems within the software categories classified above. A five-category Likert scale was used for this question with the extremes "very significant" and "very insignificant". Figure 35 illustrates how often the categories "very significant" and "significant" were chosen. For reasons of simplification, the figure does not show the answers in the other categories.

In general, enterprises in the United States seem to be more likely to experience problems of incompatibility than in Germany. The largest differences appear in the categories of *business software, e-mail programs* and *programming languages*.

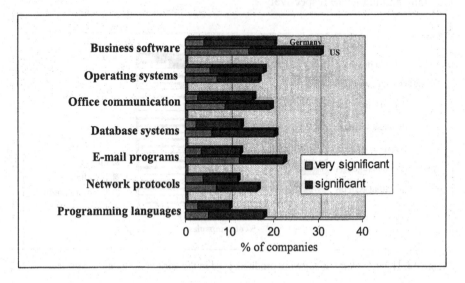

Figure 35: The problem of incompatibility.

MIS managers in both countries report their largest problems of incompatibility in the area of *business software*. This is likely to be a result of the strategic importance of such systems in enterprises. Nowadays, business software has an impact on all key processes. Therefore, incompatibilities in this area lead to more significant problems than in other areas.

Assuming that the chance of incompatibility problems increases with the number of different products in use, the correlation between these two variables was measured. It was necessary to consider that the variable that measures the number of different standards is an interval variable, while the incompatibility problems were measured ordinally. In this case, it is appropriate to apply statistical tests for the ordinal level. Therefore, the interval variable was transferred to an ordinal scale. To do this, the six categories "1 product in use", "2 products in use", "3 products in use", "4 products in use", "5 products in use" and "more than 5 products in use" were created. Then the Goodman's and Kruskal's Gamma and the Spearman's Rank-Order Correlation Coefficient (rho) were calculated. Both of them are applicable to measuring the correlation of ordinal variables (Levin &

Fox, 1997). In this case the Goodman's and Kruskal's Gamma is a particularly appropriate measure of correlation, since the variables involved are ranked in categories (Levin & Fox, 1997, 331). In Table 17 the measured values of gamma and rho are displayed whenever the level of significance (α) was better than 0.05, since a α larger then 0.05 would be statistically questionable.

Table 17: The correlation between incompatibility and the number of different standards/ products used.

	Goodman's and Kruskal's Gamma				Spearman's rho			
	Germany		US		Germany		US	
	gam-ma	α	gam-ma	α	rho	α	rho	α
Office communication	.301	.000	.371	.003	.244	.000	.305	.004
Database software	.295	.000	.252	.013	.276	.000	.241	.025
Business software	**.459**	**.000**	**.428**	**.000**	**.408**	**.000**	**.422**	**.000**
E-mail programs	.382	.000	.463	.000	.261	.000	.361	.000
Network protocols	.369	.000			.312	.000		
Programming languages	.310	.000			.289	.000		
Operation Systems	.315	.000			.294	.000		

In most of the cases there is a moderate positive correlation between the two variables. For the German data sample, in every software category all levels of significance for both coefficients are better than 0.0005 (SPSS shows the value .000). This means that with a confidence of more than 99.95 percent the measured correlation is not a result of sampling error.

The empty spaces in the table indicate the areas in which α is larger than 0.05 and therefore correlations are not significant. This applies for the categories *network protocols, programming languages,* and *operation systems* in the US sample. One reason for this might be that this sample is smaller than the German one. However, in general, a positive correlation was found between the problem of incompatibility and the number of different software standards used.

There is a particularly strong correlation in the category of *business software.* Taking into consideration the fact that the MIS managers also reported this category as the one with the largest problem of incompatibility, it seems reasonable to reduce potential incompatibilities by reducing the number of different products used in the company. Taking the question of centralization and decentralization into account, the example of business software will later be used to analyze further whether centralization can reduce the number of different products in use and therefore reduce incompatibility problems.

The results show that software incompatibilities are an important matter in today's enterprises and that the decision problem described by the standardization models is of high practical relevance.

4.3.4.2 Case Study: Guidelines for Standardization and Migration at Lufthansa AG

To coordinate the use of software products and to ensure compatibility within the Lufthansa group mandatory standards are set in various IT areas. Generally, the central MIS department (Konzern-Informationsmanagement, KIM) develops IT strategies and submits standardization proposals to the Information Management Board (IM-Board) consisting of the chairman of the KIM and the MIS managers of all Lufthansa companies. The IM-Board passes the standards, which are published and then become mandatory after a certain migration period. Figure 36 shows an organizational chart of the information management at Lufthansa.

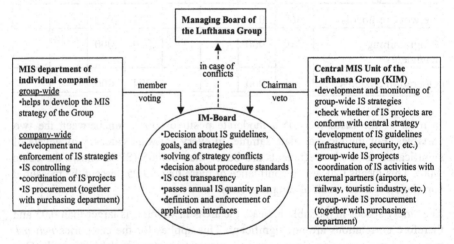

Figure 36: Lufthansa Information Management

To *standardize the process of standardization* the KIM developed guidelines of standardization and migration (Lufthansa Konzern-Informationsmanagement 1998a, 1998b) which are described in the following. They build a framework for the detailed standardization rules published by the IM board.

Guidelines for Standardization

The KIM refers to a *standard* to as an effective rule in the area of information technology. Table 18 shows the areas of standardization with a priority classification.

Table 18: Areas of standardization and their priorities at Lufthansa.

	Classi-fication		Classi-fication
system architectures and products		**methods and procedures**	
communication		LAN operating concept	A
email	A	security	A
news groups	A	cryptography	A
video conferencing	B	authorization	B
Internet chat	B	strategic information planning	A
business TV	C	project management	A
push technology	C	stock management	B
information viewing	A	address schema (mail)	A
coordination			
calendaring and scheduling	A	**application architectures and products**	
cooperation		Enterprise Resource Planning (SAP)	A
authoring, presentation, publishing (office productivity)	A		
		data and information architectures	
authoring, archiving (document management)	B	content structure of the Intranet	A
information retrieval	A		

Table 18: (continued)

systems		hardware architectures and products	
client operating systems	A	PC hardware	A
server operating systems	A		
network operating systems	A	**A:** high standardization priority since the technology is already in wide-spread use within Lufthansa	
network protocols	A		
other systems		**B:** middle standardization priority since the technology is only used in certain areas	
data bases	A		
directories	A		
mail servers	A	**C:** no standardization priority since the technology will not be used within the planning horizon.	
mail protocols	A		
application server	B	**D:** no standardization needed since the use of the technology at Lufthansa is not planned for the future	
system management	B		

Generally, standards in the different areas are not set by naming certain software products or brands, but by defining the format which has to be used to exchange data and information with communication partners within Lufthansa. For example, the Microsoft Word 97-format has been the standard for the document exchange in the area of text processing since 1998. Lufthansa employees are free to use any product they like as long as the documents they exchange are Microsoft Word 97 compatible.

The primary goal of standardization is the long-term reduction of Total Costs of Ownership (TCO) within the Lufthansa group. The basic idea of TCO was developed by the Gardner Group a few years ago. The model considers all the costs, benefits, and values of buying, owning, and using IT components (*life cycle costs*). Thus, not only start up costs, but also all subsequent costs are considered, e.g. for administration, technical support, or using the solution (Renn/Guptill 1998). Another goal is smooth communication, coordination, and cooperation in a networked environment especially within the Lufthansa group. An additional objective is to realize economies of scale in the purchasing department as well as to limit the excessive dependency on certain suppliers or technologies.

Standards become mandatory for all companies which are owned by Lufthansa by more than 50%. For these subsidiaries, individual IT-standardization has to be in harmony with the overall central strategy. All (geographical, technical, or organizational) areas which are excepted from this rule must be made clear in a supplement to the relevant standardization rule. Sometimes restricted areas of standardization may be defined (e.g. if standards are only effective for the Star Alliance).

Standardization must be moderate, interfering as little as possible with the individual needs of the users. For this reason standards are published and become mandatory on a certain date (the default is 6 months after publication). If possible only architectures and interfaces should be regulated by standards. If practicable, existing widespread de-facto standards are to be considered.

Standards for the Lufthansa group are statements of direction. Activities aimed at reaching conformity with the standards within the defined migration period are to start once these rules are published. Nevertheless, a complete, immediate migration is not necessary; the continuity of operative business must be taken into consideration.

To ensure the success of standardization activities, the individual subsidiaries should participate in the benefits of the group-wide standardization instead of just being forced to obey the rules. In cooperation with the Institute of Information Systems at J. W. Goethe-University, Frankfurt, the central MIS department of Lufthansa is analyzing whether the standardization models described above and the TCO approach might be appropriate for the evaluation of standardization benefits and costs, and how reallocation of resources might help to support efficient standardization. In the area of standardizing directory services, a similar cooperation with Siemens AG was successful (Weitzel/Son/Westarp/Buxmann/ König 2000).

Standardization is not seen as a discrete event, but a process. This process needs to be formalized, based on sufficient information, future oriented, technical approved, transparent, and consensus oriented (i.e. only if there is no consensus within the IM board does the management board decide). At Lufthansa the MIS department is responsible for supporting the process of standardization by an effective information and coordination policy.

Guidelines for Migration

The central MIS department of Lufthansa (KIM) refers to *migration* as the planning and execution of measures to transform a part of the IT infrastructure from an actual state to a target state. In the context of standardization this means the planning and execution of measures leading to conformity with the mandatory central IS standards. After the standards are published, the affected departments or companies have to start immediately with the relevant migration which has to be completed by the end of the defined migration period. As mentioned above, this period is usually 6 months, the maximum being 18 months. Because of extremely short product cycles in the software industry, the MIS department generally strives for shorter migration intervals.

The planning of measures aimed at reaching conformity with the published standards is carried out by every company of Lufthansa individually. It depends on their specific technical and organizational circumstances. The written migration plan has to contain the *migration path* defining the sequence of steps leading to conformity, the *migration schedule* defining matters of time, and the *migration environment* consisting of information about technical procedures and tools used for the migration.

Certain principles for migration are defined. The coexistence of old and new products(/standards) is allowed during the migration interval. Generally, a user of the new standard has to ensure compatibility with communication partners within Lufthansa, *before* the migration period ends, whereas *afterwards*, users of the old standard are responsible for being compatible.

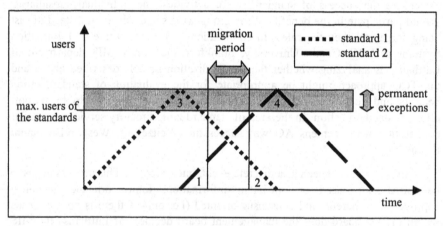

Figure 37: The Migration of IT-Standards at Lufthansa.

There are generally three kinds of exceptions to the centrally set standardization rules, marked by the triangles (1-4) in Figure 37.

1. The standard is used before it was officially published by the central MIS department. Because of specific organizational or technical circumstances it might be necessary for a Lufthansa subsidiary or department to switch to a new technology although the relevant standard has not yet been published (triangle 1). In this case, exceptions are possible. An example was Lufthansa Cargo GmbH, which was allowed to switch to the Microsoft Word 97-standard early.

2. If for important reasons it is impossible to switch to the new standard in time, the old technology might be allowed even after the standardization rules have become mandatory (triangle 2).

3. Technical or organizational restrictions might be a reason for totally exempting departments or whole companies of Lufthansa from standardization (triangles 3 and 4).

The particular company of the Lufthansa group has to apply for an exception well in advance. The application has to contain the justification for the exception and a plan for how the negative impact on others can be minimized. Three reasons for an exception are acceptable:

1. External partners (customers, suppliers, etc.) require a certain technology or product (pressure from business partners).

2. The existence of custom-made software systems/modules with specific requirements. Some Lufthansa companies have very complicated systems with large parts of custom-made modules integrated with standard software (e.g. Lufthansa Service Holding, see Westarp/Weitzel/Margaritis/Buxmann/König 2000).

3. Test and evaluation of new technologies which might later become a standard for the whole group.

If exceptions are granted, the particular company is responsible for trouble-free communication with other subsidiaries and has to bear any additional costs in this context. Exceptions can only be temporary. The company has to make clear how conformity with the standards can be achieved in the long run. For products which come within the scope of exception agreements no central support services (e.g. training) can be offered.

The standardization and migration rules of the Lufthansa group show that the MIS management of large companies is aware of the need to standardize the use of software solutions. They also demonstrate an approach to handling the data, complexity, and implementation problem. Nevertheless, it becomes clear that it is difficult for central MIS units to collect data about the costs and benefits of using software solutions.

4.3.4.3 Centralized and Decentralized Networks

The simulations of Buxmann, Weitzel, and König (1999) show a standardization gap between centralized and decentralized coordinated communication networks. This means that centrally coordinated networks should have fewer compatibility problems. In this section, empirical studies of the fortune1000 companies in Germany and the US will be used to evaluate these findings. Proposing the hypothesis that centralization leads to more homogeneous software solutions (for the field of business software), the potential correlations between centralization of decision-making and number of different products used were measured (for the data samples of both countries).

The respondents were asked to answer the question: who makes the decision in the field of business software? To answer this question the respondents could choose from the following categories:

1. company management

2. head/employee of the central MIS department

3. head/employee of an operating department (e.g. controlling, accounting)

4. head/employee of a business unit

5. other

Multiple answers were possible. For analysis and interpretation the data was regrouped. Answers of category 1 and 2 were classified as "central", 3 and 4 as "decentralized". Whenever answers were found in both of these groups, they were newly classified as "team". Answers were also counted under the variable "team", whenever it was explicitly mentioned in the category "others" that decisions were made with central and decentralized units participating. The table below shows the proportion (in percent) of how decisions concerning business software are currently made.

Table 19: Who decides about the implementation of business software?

in % of companies	decentralized	team	central
Germany	3.3	56.7	40
US	8.5	61.7	29.8

In most of the cases, decisions concerning the selection of business software are made within teams, i.e. both central IT departments and decentralized departments are involved in the decision process. An interesting result, however, is that in Germany decision-making is currently more often centrally organized.

It appears to be promising to take a closer look at a potential connection between the greater degree of centralization (see Table 17) and the smaller heterogeneity (see Figure 34) in Germany in comparison to the United States. In accordance with the results of the numerical simulation, centralization (see Figure 29) seems to lead to more homogenous solutions. This correlation appears to be reasonable since a central decision- making unit is able to consider company-wide network effects related to the use of software standards. This hypothesis was empirically evaluated by using business software as an example. In order to do this, the potential correlation between *centralization of decision making* and *number of different products used* (the latter as an indicator for the degree of standardization) was measured for the data samples of both countries. To measure potential correlation between the two variables the *Goodman's and Kruskal's Gamma* and the *Spearman's Rank-Order Correlation Coefficient (rho)* were calculated. Table 20 shows the results.

Table 20: The correlation between the degree of centralization and the number of different products used.

Goodman's and Kruskal's Gamma				Spearman's rho			
Germany		US		Germany		US	
gamma	α	gamma	α	rho	α	rho	α
-.053	.637	-.388	.006	-.036	.633	-.307	.010

While for the German sample no significant correlation was found, testing the US sample shows a moderate, statistically significant, and negative correlation between the number of different products in use and the degree of centralization. Therefore, the research hypothesis can be accepted for the US sample: The number of different types of business software used in enterprises decreases when the degree of centralization increases.

These results substantiate the findings of Buxmann/Weitzel/König (1999) showing that centralization leads to more standardization and therefore to fewer problems of incompatibility. Nevertheless, the measured correlation needs further examination since it could statistically only be proven in the comparatively small US sample.

The empirical analysis shows that the differences between standardization decisions in centralized and decentralized information networks exist in the real world. This substantiates the approach to describing the two situations in different models. Nevertheless, the models do not offer the possibility of considering centrality endogenously. Centrality in terms of the structural (topological) position within an information network, or centrality in terms of decision power or other influences of individual nodes on others cannot directly be analyzed. Centralized and decentralized models seem to be a good basis for analyzing the efficiency of coordinating mechanisms. Different designs can be compared to the optimum solution calculated by the centralized model. In fact, this model has already been used as a controlling instrument to discover cost and benefit structures of communication standards like X.500 Directory Services in cooperative business networks (Weitzel/Son/Westarp/Buxmann/König 2000).

4.3.4.4   Model Parameter

After analyzing the empirical relevance of the standardization models and their findings, this section focuses on their parameters and the data needed. The studies in section 0 show that the data needed for the parameters of the standardization models can be collected empirically for some software products, while it is difficult for others. Generally, the companies seem to have a good overview of the costs and benefits in the area of EDI. The costs of EDI solutions consist of "node-related" costs, such as start-up costs and running costs for the solution, and "edge-related" costs, such as setting up a new communication partner. Focusing on the benefits, the same distinction can be found. The main benefits derive from "edge-related" benefits, such as savings per order or invoice. Additionally, better warehouse management leading to reduced stock value is one of the "node-related" benefits. Focusing more on the communication between departments or subsidiaries within a company or a company group, a similar structure can be found for ERP systems. Costs of implementing and running the system are amortized by the benefits of compatibility between the communicating departments. Nevertheless, the studies reveal that, while costs can be estimated more or less precisely, it is much harder to measure the benefits of ERP systems. As regards office communication software, the Lufthansa case study shows the effort to consider subsequent costs for administration and technical support as well (Total Cost of Ownership), in an area where these costs are not easy to measure. In this case it is also interesting that it is difficult for the central MIS management to get an overview of how many MS Office licenses are bought within the company, since the departments or subsidiaries have a choice of alternative suppliers. While the benefits of compatibility are again hard to measure, the Lufthansa case study, as well as the standardization and migration guides, give a hint about how companies deal with the disadvantages of incompatibility: Before the critical migration date, the early adopters have to bear the costs of transforming their documents into the standard format, after the date, the responsibility shifts to the late adopters.

Looking at the figures of different companies, great heterogeneity in terms of the costs and savings realized can be found. This also implies that different companies benefit differently from using the same standard in information networks. Large companies have an especially strong interest in standardization, since they have the largest potential savings due to the high data volume. The case studies show that such companies try to influence their business partners to switch to the desirable software standard. One the one hand, the support of certain standards becomes a critical factor for choosing new business partners (see cases of 3Com, Karstadt, Woolworth). On the other hand, existing partners are "forced" to use the right software (see cases of 3Com, Heraeus, also Figure 11). Some companies even try to convince others to switch to another solution by transferring know-how or even sharing the costs of implementation (see case of Woolworth). This influence by some participants in information networks on the standardization decisions of others (by power, their central position in the network, monetary incentives, or other support) cannot be modeled with the existing standardization models.

4.3.4.5 Summary of the Evaluation

The benefits and restrictions of the centralized and decentralized standardization models can be summarized as follows.

The models are a good basis for describing real world standardization problems in centralized and decentralized information networks such as companies or business networks, respectively in general terms. Describing the trade-off between node-related standardization costs and edge-related savings the models can help to reveal costs and benefits structures. Since the centralized model reveals the optimum set of standards (first-best solution) it can be used as a controlling instrument for standardization decisions in networks. In addition, the decentralized model is very useful for describing the possible coordination mechanisms for networks with independent participants and individual standardization decisions. The comparison of the two mechanisms offers a valuable instrument for evaluating the efficiency of decentralized systems and to what extent centralization (e.g. by public intervention) might be favorable. The empirical study and the case studies show that the standardization problem exists within and between companies. They also verify the "standardization gap" between centralized and decentralized coordination. The example of intermediation shows that the models can be modified to some extent to consider other important determinants of standardization in communication networks.

Nevertheless, the models are neither sufficient to describe the dynamics and the variety of diffusion processes in software markets, nor are they a good basis for analyzing the marketing strategies of software vendors.

The information assumptions of the centralized model are generally rather unrealistic, resulting in various problems (Buxmann/Weitzel/König 1999). First of all, the assumption that a central node has knowledge about the entire costs and benefits structure of the network leads to the data problem. Participants in networks might have incentives to lie about their real costs and benefits. Furthermore, the empirical studies show that it is difficult for the participants to estimate the relevant figures, especially the standardization benefits. Finally, in large networks like whole markets, the cost of collecting the data needed for the model is prohibitive. Secondly, a complexity problem exists. Calculation of the first-best solution becomes extremely difficult in larger networks with different standards to choose from. This is the reason why the simulations of the centralized model were conducted with networks with a maximum of 20 participants and a maximum of 5 different standards. Of course these network sizes are far too small to be a benchmark for real markets. Third, the case studies show that even in hierarchical organizations a central coordinating unit has problems in controlling the implementation of the first-best solution (implementation problem).

The decentralized model does not assume an omniscient central unit. It is based on more realistic assumptions, taking the bounded rationality of actors into account. It offers the opportunity of testing various decentralized coordination designs in comparison with the optimum solution. Nevertheless, the problem of data collection still remains, especially for large networks.

As the extension of the centralized model by considering intermediaries showed, it is generally also possible to integrate determinants of decisions on standards in communication networks other than the standardization costs and savings alone. Nevertheless, the extension also demonstrated that the models become rather complicated and difficult to handle, especially when the data problem is taken into account. Whether the heterogeneous determinants of software markets can be considered by extending the models is therefore questionable.

Considering the approaches for diffusion processes in markets produces additional problems. The basis of the models is fully connected networks. Like the concept of the installed base in network effect literature (see section 5.2), for the centralized model this leads to the results that simulations often show situations in which one standard dominates the market (Buxmann 1996, 86-96), while the coexistence of standards is unlikely. For the decentralized model first steps towards structural patterns other than the fully connected graph already exist. Nevertheless, the models do not offer a basis for modeling important determinants of diffusion in software markets like structural patterns of communication networks (density, connectivity, topology, etc.), price segments, heterogeneity of preferences, standardization pressure from strong business partners, etc. The models are designed more as coordination instruments to optimize standardization decisions in small communication networks, rather than to simulate the diffusion processes of various competing software products in markets. Furthermore, the models do not offer much help for analyzing different software markets and designing adequate marketing strategies for vendors.

5 Diffusion of Innovations and Network Effect Theory

As described, standardization models focus rather on modeling the individual's decision-making and the efficiency of centralized and decentralized coordination mechanisms than on dynamic processes in markets.

Searching for appropriate instruments to model the software market, two other areas of research seem to be promising. On the one hand, *models of the diffusion of innovations* focus on explaining and forecasting the process of the adoption of innovations over time. On the other hand, *theory of positive network effects* analyzes the specific characteristics of markets for network effects goods (such as software products).

In the following, the broad area of existing diffusion models will first be examined. The analysis focuses on economic models of innovation diffusion and on network models of diffusion. Secondly, existing approaches derived from the theory of positive network effects are examined. It is shown that the assumptions and simplifications implicitly used for modeling adoption processes fail to explain the real-world variety of diffusion courses in today's dynamic IT markets. Since many of the examined concepts rely on the neo-classical approach, the general deficiencies of this paradigm are also revealed in the end of this section.

Identifying requirements for a more general model of network effect markets, the results will build the basis for the simulation model of software markets introduced in section 6.

5.1   Diffusion Models

5.1.1   Diffusion of Innovations in Economic Literature

The term diffusion is generally defined as *"the process by which an innovation is communicated through certain channels over time among the members of a social system"* (Rogers 1983, 5). The traditional economic analysis of diffusion focuses on describing and forecasting the adoption of products in markets. In particular, the question of which factors influence the speed and specific course of diffusion processes arises (Weiber 1993). Traditional diffusion models are based on similar assumptions: Generally, the number of new adopters in a certain period of time is modeled as the proportion of the group of market participants that have not yet adopted the innovation. If M is the cumulative number of potential adopters and N^*_{t-1} is the cumulative number of adopters until period $t-1$ then the number of adopters of a certain innovation in period t can be expressed by the following differential equation:

$$N_t = g_t (M - N^*_{t-1})$$

The term $g_t = N_t / (M - N^*_{t-1})$ can then be interpreted as the coefficient of diffusion describing the relationship between the rate of diffusion and the number of potential adopters existing at t. Most of the traditional approaches aim at revealing the specific value of g_t which depends on the nature of the innovation, communication channels, and social system attributes (Mahajan/Peterson 1985, 14). It is common to describe the coefficient of diffusion as a function of the cumulative adopters, which can generally be referred to as $g_t = a + b \cdot N^*_{t-1}$. Based on this fundamental structure, three different types of diffusion models are most common (Weiber 1993, Lilien/Kotler 1983, 706-740, Mahajan/Peterson 1985, 12-26):

Exponential diffusion model:
$$N_t = a \cdot (M - N^*_{t-1})$$

Logistic diffusion model:
$$N_t = b \cdot N^*_{t-1} (M - N^*_{t-1})$$

Semilogistic diffusion model:
$$N_t = a \cdot (M - N^*_{t-1}) + b \cdot N^*_{t-1} (M - N^*_{t-1})$$

The *exponential diffusion model* (also *external influence model* or *pure innovative model*) assumes that the number of new adopters is determined by influences from outside the system, e.g. mass communication.

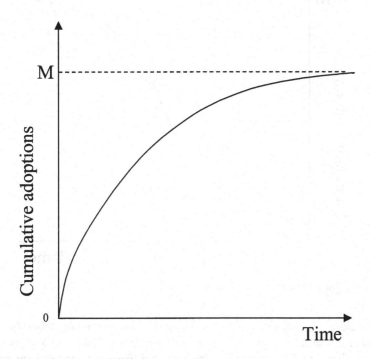

Figure 38: Typical exponential diffusion curve.

The *logistic diffusion model* (also *internal influence model* or *pure imitative model*) assumes that the decision to become a new adopter is determined solely by the positive influence of existing adopters (e.g. word of mouth).

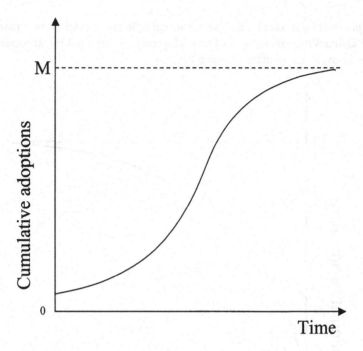

Figure 39: Typical logistic diffusion curve.

The *semilogistic diffusion model* (also *mixed influence model*) considers both internal and external influences. A famous example of the latter is the *Bass model*, which has been used for forecasting innovation diffusion in various areas such as retail service, industrial technology, agricultural, educational, pharmaceutical, and consumer durable goods markets (Bass 1969, Mahajan/Muller/Bass 1990, 2).

Despite the existence of many different applications of these diffusion models (for a comprehensive overview of the traditional diffusion models refer to Gierl 1987, Mahajan/Muller/Bass 1990), the approaches are not sufficient to model the diffusion of network effect products. Schoder 1995 names three areas of deficit (Schoder 1995, 46-50). First of all, there is a lack of analysis concerning the phenomenon of critical mass. Furthermore, the traditional diffusion models cannot explain the variety of diffusion courses. In the context of software products, the models cannot deal with the heterogeneous properties of different markets like ERP systems, EDI solutions, or office communication software, which lead to completely different diffusion patterns. Third, the models do not sufficiently consider the interaction of potential adopters within their socio-economic environment, how adoption changes their relationship with other participants in the system, and how the willingness to pay a certain price changes with adoption within a certain group. Additionally, the models do not sufficiently support the analysis of competing products in a market, which of course is highly relevant in network effect markets. Therefore, it is not surprising that the broad acceptance of logistic and semilogistic approaches is found in areas where innovations have only small consumer interdependencies, where the acceleration of the adoption is characteristically slow, and where the diffusion function is similar to normal distribution (Schoder 1995, 48-49). All of these requirements are rather unrealistic for software markets.

5.1.2 Network Models of the Diffusion of Innovations

Besides the economic research approaches described above, many (mostly empirical) studies of diffusion processes can be found in various research areas such as anthropology, early sociology, rural sociology, education, medical sociology, communication, etc. (for an early overview of existing empirical studies refer to Rogers/Shoemaker 1971, 44-96). Most of the models are based on the *threshold* and *critical mass* approaches which analyze the diffusion rate of innovations, collective behavior, or public opinion (e.g. Granovetter 1978, Marwell/Oliver/Prahl 1988). A long research tradition exists in the area of *network models of diffusion of innovations*. Mainly relying on empirical analysis, this field has a long tradition in various fields. Complementing the analysis of diffusion of innovations, network analysis in this context is an instrument for analyzing the pattern of interpersonal communication in a social network (for concepts of geographical network analysis e.g. refer to Kansky 1963 or Haggett/Cliff/Frey 1977; for concepts of sociological network analysis e.g. refer to Jansen 1999).

Two early studies can be seen as the starting point for network diffusion analysis (Valente 1995, 4-15). Collecting network and diffusion data in 1955 and 1956 Coleman, Katz, and Menzel studied the diffusion of a drug innovation (tetracycline) in four towns (Coleman/Menzel/Katz 1957). With the aim of determining the role of social networks, the doctors were asked to name doctors from whom they most frequently sought discussion, friendship, and advice, respectively. The following table gives an overview of the history of this research area. The studies proved that network patterns and the characteristics of the participants influenced the diffusion process significantly. For example, the diffusion of the new drug was faster among doctors with an integrated position in the network than among isolated doctors. Another influential study was that of Rogers and Beal (1958), who collected data from farmers on the social network and on the adoption time of various farm innovations. Again the influence of networks was proven.

In general, network diffusion models can be divided into *relational models* and *structural models*. Relational models analyze how direct contacts between participants in networks influence the decision to adopt or not adopt an innovation. In contrast, structural models focus on the pattern of all relationships and show how the structural characteristics of a social system determine the diffusion process. Table 21 shows common concepts of these models (Valente 1995, 31-61).

Table 21: Concepts of relational and structural diffusion network models.

Relational Diffusion Network Models	Structural Diffusion Network Models
• opinion leadership • group membership • personal network density • personal network exposure	• centrality • position equivalence • structural equivalence (Burt 1987)

The *opinion leadership* concept assumes that some individuals in networks have a strong influence on the adoption decisions of many others (see for an early approach: Coleman/Menzel/Katz 1957).

This approach is the foundation of market penetration strategies such as the two-step flow strategy where vendors first influence opinion leaders in a market who then influence their opinion followers.

The concept of *group membership* analyzes the relevance of intra-group pressure towards conformity.

Personal network density measures the interconnectedness of an individual's network. A network is dense if the communication partners of an individual also communicate with each other. A dense network is also called integrated, while a network with low density is referred to as radial (Figure 40).

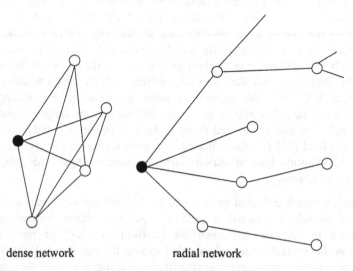

dense network   radial network

Figure 40: A dense and a radial interpersonal network (Valente 1995, 41).

If density is measured for the whole network, it is common to divide the total number of existing links T by the number of the maximum possible number of links. With n participants in a symmetrical network, the latter is $n(n-1)/2$, for an asymmetrical network it is $n(n-1)$. This leads to the following measures of network density:

<u>Density of a symmetrical network</u>

$$D_s = \frac{T}{n(n-1)/2}$$

<u>Density of an asymmetrical network</u>

$$D_a = \frac{T}{n(n-1)}$$

When designing the simulation model in section 6, which will be based on an asymmetrical network structure, the latter measure will be referred to as the *connectivity*.

Personal network exposure is a measure of how intensely an individual is exposed to an innovation, i.e. how many of their network links lead to an adopter of a certain innovation. Figure 41 shows the concept by using data from the medical innovation study of Coleman, Katz, and Menzel (1966). In time period 1 no one had yet adopted the innovation, the exposure was 0. Over time, the number of adopters (black circles) directly linked to the individual in the middle increased, thus the exposure increased. Finally, in period 8, all doctors in the personal communication network had adopted the innovation, resulting in an exposure of 100%. The connection to the concept of threshold (e.g. Granovetter 1978) is obvious. The threshold of an individual is their exposure at the time of adoption (Valente 1995, 44).

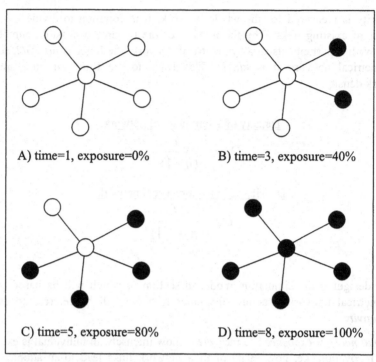

A) time=1, exposure=0%   B) time=3, exposure=40%

C) time=5, exposure=80%   D) time=8, exposure=100%

Figure 41: Personal network exposure to an innovation (Valente 1995, 44).

In the literature, various centrality measures exist for individuals and for the whole network (Freeman 1979, Bolland 1988).

Looking at these concepts, the field of diffusion network analysis seems to be a valuable aid to modeling software markets. In contrast to the fundamental diffusion models, the structure and characteristics of communication networks, shown to be relevant for decisions on software by the empirical studies outlined above (e.g. strong influence of some business partners, centralized decisions in company groups, differences in the intensity of communication, etc.), are taken into account. Nevertheless, especially in the context of the research objective of this work, deficiencies can be identified. On the one hand, the current models lack a systematic identification of those network characteristics that are relevant for network effect markets like software markets. Most of the studies refer to empirical data sets using specific networks as examples. An approach to generating networks of different topologies to systematically test how variations of single or a set of network characteristics changes diffusion processes of network effect goods is still needed. Even common network analysis software such as Negopy (Richards 1995) need to be fed with complete data sets of networks to perform their calculations. The simulation model introduced in section 6 aims at closing this gap. The objective is to integrate those concepts of network analysis that are relevant for software markets with other relevant models of network effect goods into one model. Therefore, the next section will take a closer look at existing approaches from the rapidly growing research field referred to as network effect theory.

5.2 Reconsidering Network Effect Theory

5.2.1 Existing Approaches

The primary goal of most traditional approaches in the area of the *theory of positive network effects* is an analysis of particular properties of modern information and communication technologies, i.e. increasing returns to marginal adopters, or network effects (e.g. Farrell/Saloner 1985, Katz/Shapiro 1985, Besen/Farrell 1994). Thus, the particularity of network effects lies in the fact that they are considered to be characteristic of IT products and standards that are therefore different in character from more traditional commodities and subject to different problems which markets cannot as readily solve (Katz/Shapiro 1985, Farrell/Saloner 1985, Arthur 1996). Various perspectives can be distinguished in the literature (Kleinemeyer 1998, Yang 1997, David/Greenstein 1990).

Looking at *empirical* approaches (Table 22), authors mainly try to prove the relevance of network effects for software (Gandal 1994, Moch 1995, Brynjolfsson/Kemerer 1996, Gröhn 1999), hardware (Hartmann/Teece 1990), or telecommunication markets (Artle/Averous 1973, Squire 1973, Economides/ Himmelberg 1995). Most of these authors assume that network effects derive from product characteristics like interfaces for data exchange with other applications. By using regression analysis to estimate the hedonic price function of network effect goods, the hypothesis that the existence of such attributes increases the willingness to pay for the relevant product is statistically proven (for a more comprehensive discussion refer to Gröhn 1996). The results indicate the relevance of product characteristics that might lead to actual network effects in the markets. Nevertheless, the analysis of network effects and their influence on market processes and the diffusion of innovations is not at the center of attention.

Table 22: Empirical approaches to model network effects goods.

	Objective	Modeling network effects
Hartmann/ Teece (1990)	hardware (observation 1976-83): hedonic price function dependent on installed base	regression, estimation of hedonic price function
Gandal (1994)	analysis of spreadsheet software (panel data 1986-91), proves the existence of network effects empirically	regression, estimation of hedonic price function
Economides /Himmelberg (1995)	analysis of fax machines (observation, census data 1979-92), estimation of equilibrium size of competing networks dependent on income and installed base, empirical evaluation of the model	installed base: $u(y,n^e)$ ▶ Consumer y has a willingness to pay of $u(y,n^e)$ for a network good with an associated expected network size of n^e.
Moch (1995)	database software (observation 1986-94): evaluation of relevant (quality and network effect) characteristics	regression, estimation of hedonic price function
Gröhn (1999)	word processing (observation of software tests in magazines 1985-95), proves the existence of network effects empirically	regression, estimation of hedonic price function
Gallaugher/ Wang (1999)	Web server (monthly observations of Windows and Unix products, August 1995-February 1997), prove of positive relation between price and market share in markets without free products, no relationship found in markets were free products dominate	regression, estimation of hedonic price function

Existing *analytical* models of positive network effects focus on individual buying decisions, marketing strategies of competing vendors, supply and demand equilibria, and welfare implications. They mostly use equilibrium analysis to explain phenomena such as the start-up problem (Rohlfs 1974, Oren/Smith 1981, Katz/Shapiro 1985, 1994, Wiese 1990, Besen/Farell 1994, Economides/Himmelberg 1995), market failure (Farrell/Saloner 1985, 1986, Katz/Shapiro 1986, 1992, 1994, Gröhn 1999), instability (also called "tippiness") of network effect markets

(Arthur 1989, 1996, Besen/Farell 1994, Farrell/Saloner 1985, Katz/Shapiro 1994, Shapiro/Varian 1998), and path dependency (David 1985, Arthur 1989, Besen/Farell 1994, Katz/Shapiro 1994, Liebowitz/Margolis 1995).

Table 23: Analytical approaches to model network effect goods.

	Objective	Modeling network effects
Rohlfs (1974)	Equilibrium analysis of network effect goods, development of cumulative demand functions	expected installed base: $$q_i^D = q_i^D(p, q_1, ..., q_{i-1}, q_{i+1}, ..., q_n)$$ ▶ The binary variable q_i takes a value of 1 if user i actually participates in the network of n actors, q_i^D describes the user's demand for participation with $q_i^D = 1$ if i wishes to participate, i.e. if participation is more advantageous to i than not to participate.
Katz/ Shapiro (1985)	Welfare (efficiency) analysis, effect of network effects on competition and market equilibrium	installed base: $$U_i = r + v(y_i^e) - p_i$$ ▶ $r + v(y_i^e)$ describes consumer i's overall willingness to pay for a product with expected network size y^e; thus, $v(y)$ is the expected value of the network effect while $v(0)=0$ and r representing a consumer's basic willingness to pay without other users.

102

Table 23: (continued)

Farrell/ Saloner (1986)	Equilibrium analysis, welfare (efficiency) analysis, excess inertia and excess momentum in case of competing technologies	installed base: $u(x) = a + bx$ ▸ Similar to "r" in Katz/Shapiro's model (1985), a denotes network-independent benefits, with u(x) describing a user's utility derived from a network of size x.
Arthur (1989)	Influence of increasing, constant, and diminishing network effects on market equilibria, relevance of path dependency	existing installed base: $a_R + rn_A$, $b_R + rn_B$ ▸ Technologies A and B compete, with actors of type R preferring A and actors of type S preferring B $(a_R > b_R \ and \ a_S < b_S)$. Network effects are determined by the number of previous adopters of the respective technology (n_A and n_B). Utility of actor of type R derived from A equals $a_R + rn_A$ and derived from B equals $b_R + rn_B$, analogous for S-preferring actors.
Wiese (1990)	Duopol simulation model for markets with network effects, price strategy as Nash equilibrium	installed base: $U^i = U^i(z_i, x_i, l)$ ▸ Utility for individual i derived from consuming z_i units of network effect good x, l describes the total number of consumers of x.

Table 23: (continued)

Church/ Gandal (1996)	Equilibrium and welfare analysis of indirect network effects, the role of software in case of incompatible competing hardware systems	network effects dependent on inter-dependencies between hard- and software, not dependent on network size
Oren/Smith/ Wilson (1982)	Optimal tariff policy for communication networks	installed base: $w(q,t,Y)$ ▸ Without network effects, $W(q,t)$ denotes a consumer's maximum willingness to pay for the first q units of consumption and t identifying consumer types. Network effects are a function of other consumers' type, $Y \subseteq [0,1]$ is the set of t indices identifying other user that have entered the network.
Dhebar/ Oren (1985, 1986)	Optimal monopolistic intertemporal pricing	installed base: $W(\eta, X)$ or $W(q,\eta,X)$ ▸ $W(\eta, X)$ denotes the willingness to pay for network effect goods for individual η and a given network size of X. Thus, p being the price for network participation, η's consumer surplus equals $(W(\eta, X) - p)$. Adding q as quantity volume, network effects are described as $W(q,\eta,X)$ monotonically increasing in X.

The following are common results:

- The existence of network effects often results in market failure, i.e. Pareto inefficiencies.

- Multiple, incompatible technologies can only rarely coexist, since network size is the most important decision criterion. This means a product with a significantly larger number of users will finally gain total market share and lock-in in to a monopoly-like situation.

- Instability is a typical characteristic of network effect markets, meaning that after one product reaches a critical number of users (*critical mass*), its diffusion process will suddenly accelerate leaving all competing products behind, which are then doomed to disappear from the market.

- The start-up problem prevents the adoption even of superior products; excess inertia can occur, i.e. the number of users is smaller than Pareto efficient, as no actor is willing to bear the over proportional risk of being among the first adopters of an innovation.

- There is a possibility that vendors will inhibit market failure and internalize the network gains which would otherwise be more or less lost, for example by strategic intertemporal pricing, i.e. low or negative prices at early periods of diffusion to attract a critical mass of adopters (*penetration strategy*). This strategy can overcome the start-up problem and excess inertia.

- The possibility of intertemporal pricing by vendors does not guarantee social optimality per se. Penetration strategy can result in excess momentum, i.e. the number of users is larger than Pareto efficient.

- The question of whether the laissez-faire of decentralized markets should be replaced by centralized state control to ensure favorable diffusion of technologies subject to network effects arises.

While the traditional models contribute greatly to the understanding of a wide variety of general problems associated with the diffusion of network effect markets, a closer look reveals various deficiencies. The examination of network effects is carried out in a rather general way. Furthermore, most of the approaches only focus on the installed base of the whole market. The specific interaction of potential adopters within their individual communication network environment is neglected. As a result, they fail to explain the variety of diffusion courses in today's dynamic software markets. Important phenomena which cannot be explained or even described using the analytical "installed base" approaches were identified by the empirical studies in section 3:

- the coexistence of different products despite strong network effects (e.g. heterogeneous EDI and ERP markets, Figure 7 and Figure 15)

- the appearance of small but stable clusters of users of a certain solution despite the fact that the competition dominates the rest of the market (e.g. Oracle Applications in the SAP dominated German market, Figure 15)

- the fact that strong players in communication networks force other participants to use a certain solution (e.g. the cases of 3Com, Karstadt, Woolworth, Deutsche Bank, and Heraeus).

5.2.2 Common Drawbacks in Traditional Network Effect Models

Conducting a more detailed analysis the following areas of common drawbacks of existing models can be distinguished:

5.2.2.1 Modeling Network Effects

The literature agrees on the relevance of positive network effects, but the examination and consideration of these effects in the models is conducted in a rather general way. Different characteristics of heterogeneous markets like ERP systems, office suites, Internet browsers, or EDI solutions and their unique dynamics are not dealt with. The simple distinction between direct and indirect network effects (introduced by Katz/Shapiro 1985) alone is not detailed enough for an analysis of demand behavior in the software market. Taking the results of the empirical survey into account, it becomes obvious that different types of direct and indirect network effects exist, and that they are evaluated differently by potential buyers, depending on the category of the software product. In contrast to the real world where communication within the individual communication network is a very important issue for decisions on software, direct network effects are considered in the utility function of individual consumers only as the aggregated number of users in a market, referred to as the *installed base*. Table 23 illustrates clearly how most of the models are based on this assumption. Personal networks in comparison with the whole market are not at the center of attention. The simulation results of section 6 will reveal the restrictions of this unrealistic assumption.

5.2.2.2 Market Failure

Many approaches argue that positive network effects lead to market failure. It is argued that due to network externalities the equilibrium network size might be smaller than the socially optimal one (Yang 1997, 11-12). In markets with strong network effects, the benefit to consumers increases with a larger network size, i.e. a larger number of other users. Nevertheless, the preferences towards the products and the evaluations of the network effects usually differ among the potential buyers, meaning that different consumers might prefer different products to dominate the whole market. Since market participants somehow fail to internalize the impact of their buying decisions on the utility level of others, the market mechanism fails (traditional economical literature refers to this as *network externalities*). With positive consumption externalities, the marginal private benefit of buying a certain product is smaller than the social benefit. Since a coordination of market participants in this context is usually impossible, the discrepancy between private and social benefit results in network sizes that are smaller than the most efficient (Gröhn 1999, 137).

In addition to *inefficient network size* it is also argued that the market might *lock-in in to an inferior technology* (Gröhn 1999, 141-146). The participants of an existing network of an old (inferior) technology resist switching to a new incompatible (superior) product because of the network effects and the switching costs (Farrell/Saloner 1985, 1986, Katz/Shapiro 1986, 1992, Arthur 1989). Collective switching to the new product again fails because of the obvious coordination problems.

The dynamics of modern software markets in particular clearly contradict the one-sidedness of these findings. New approaches which explicitly refer to software markets argue that not all network effects are externalities (Liebowitz/Margolis 1999 or 1994, 1995a). Although an individual product-adopting actor is not likely to internalize his positive network effects on other users of a certain product, there is no essential obstacle to a vendor's (more generally owner of property rights in a technology) internalizing these effects. Especially in the case of competing products in a market, it can be argued that network effects do not necessarily imply market failure, but that there is a need for new marketing strategies for vendors to survive in or enter these markets (Liebowitz/Margolis 1999, Shapiro/Varian 1998). It becomes obvious that traditional microeconomic models as well as large areas of marketing theory need to be reconsidered. Some of the important implications of positive network effects on marketing strategies will be addressed in section 7.

5.2.2.3   The Bigger the Better

Closely related to modeling network effects as the installed base of the whole market is the proposition of indefinitely increasing positive network effects (see literature from Table 23). Multiple networks, i.e. stable user groups of competing products, are unlikely to exist if network effects are not exhaustible. This implies natural monopolies. This is contradicted by real world markets (the empirical results show heterogeneity in the markets for ERP systems and EDI solutions. Even though software is less subject to physical limitations (law of diminishing returns), there might be organizational or managerial problems restraining optimal network size (Radner 1992). The restrictions of assuming indefinite positive network effects become even more obvious if the importance of individual communication networks is taken into account. It seems unrealistic that the use of Microsoft Office in China has any direct relevance for my buying decision, or that the use of a certain EDI standard in the automobile industry has an effect on decisions in the medical sector. In this context, it is important to remember that neither positive consumption interdependencies (e.g. Leibenstein 1950) nor economies of scale on the vendors side are the subject of positive network effect literature, but that the focus is on network effects deriving from the need for compatibility (Yang 1997, 2-7).

5.2.2.4   Homogeneous Network Effects

Another limiting assumption is that of similar and actor-independent valuation of networks and growth of network effects. Heterogeneity of preferences can have a substantial impact on the evaluation of different competing networks as well as on the value assigned to new actors. Even if actors communicate within the same network and therefore gain positive network effects, the value of such effects can significantly differ in value. For example, a close friend or family member will add more value to my network than a colleague from another department of my company. It will be shown later (section 6) how group membership leads to concentration on one product within the group (due to social pressure towards conformity), but also leads to heterogeneity of products within the whole market.

In contrast to the assumption of homogeneous network effects, in real world networks actors also differ in the *extent* to which they influence the buying decisions of others. Firstly, there might be an underlying more or less hierarchical organizational structure in communication networks. An obvious example of this is centrally coordinated communication networks like those in large companies (see model of section 4.1). Central units at Lufthansa and Deutsche Bank, for example, strongly influence the product decisions of business units within the corporation to enforce compatibility (see cases of section 3). But one can also find such dependencies between otherwise independent actors like vendors and suppliers within business networks. For example, 3Com was forced to use a certain EDI standard by a large business partner, and Karstadt put pressure on its suppliers to implement an EDI system. Also, Heraeus was pressured into using a certain ERP system. In contrast to the fully connected network graph of traditional models (resulting from the concept of the *installed base*), individual actors can also have greater influence (they "produce" more network effects) simply by having a larger number of connections than other participants (similar to the concept of opinion leadership, which will be described later; see section 6). Traditional models do offer the possibility of modeling the properties of individual network participants or groups.

5.2.2.5   Costs of Network Size

If optimal networks under network externalities are monopolies, all networks are too small. This hypothesis only holds under constant or falling (average) costs of adding new members to a network. The costs of network size are ignored in almost all models. Thus network effects are not sufficient for a natural monopoly, and one single standard is not a compulsory social optimum. Instead, there can be optimum network sizes smaller than the entire population and different standards can coexist.

5.2.2.6 Centralized and Decentralized Decision Making

Different instances of coordination problems concerning the interdependencies between buying decisions are subject to different institutional backgrounds. There has to be a distinction between centralized and decentralized coordinated networks. While buying decisions in centralized networks are also determined by positive network effects, the coordination of the interdependencies is completely different. The focus must be on effective methods of finding the optimum set of standards (from an network-wide perspective) and developing the right incentive structures (reporting and distribution of the benefits of conformity; see section 4).

Most of the existing approaches analyze decentralized coordinated networks (markets). They imply that network effects cannot be internalized by independent market participants due to prohibitive coordination costs. Coordination patterns that reduce or solve the coordination problem, like cooperative behavior in groups, strong influence by single players in networks, the role of intermediaries, etc. are not considered. There is also no analysis of whether new information and communication technology like the Internet, which generally improves the power of decentralized coordination, might help to internalize positive network effects in markets. Especially if the goal is to develop appropriate marketing strategies to influence the coordination in markets, these points have to be taken into account.

5.2.2.7 Normative Implications

Closely related to the problem of designing advantageous coordination designs is the need for normative results. Whether or not public intervention is necessary in network effect markets is a common controversy in the literature. Recommendations vary from centralized standard setting or restriction of market power by the government on the one hand, to total laissez-faire without intervention on the other. Since network effects do not stop at national borders, the question of whether public intervention might be outdated arises. New emerging phenomena like the Internet show the power of decentralized coordination, while the basic implications of network effects remain the same. Despite this, no approaches to improving decentralized coordination of standardization - especially in the context of particular groups of individuals, e.g. within enterprises - can be found in the traditional models. Finding advantageous coordination designs, efficient intermediaries and network specific cost and incentive structures may lead the way to answering questions like that of the optimum network size, the trade-off between architectural (open) standards like XML and - based upon these - (proprietary) complementary technologies.

5.2.3 General Drawbacks of the Neo-Classical Paradigm

Thus most traditional approaches towards diffusion processes in standards fail to properly consider the costs and character of network effects, and lack consideration of actor contingent knowledge and of institutional personal neighborhood structures.

Although individual utility maximization, as unanimously agreed upon throughout the neoclassical paradigm, should not be disputed here, the "homo oeconomicus" comes with further premises, which the economic literature on network effects quoted above implicitly assumes him to hold. What these premises are and which of them may default within an interdisciplinary context, will be discussed in what follows.

However, if (and only if) all of these premises hold, then the validity of the following two so-called "fundamental theorems of welfare economics" (Hildenbrand/Kirman 1976) can be proven:

- A competitive total *equilibrium* always represents a *Pareto optimum allocation* of the total bundle of economic goods (a so-called Pareto optimum).

- For *each* realizable Pareto optimum a (positive) *price vector* exists, for which this Pareto optimum represents a competitive equilibrium.

The goal of an economy is thus to reach a Pareto-optimum allocation of goods (an allocation x is considered to be Pareto-optimum if and only if no other allocation y exists, which is weakly preferred over x by all individuals and strongly preferred by at least one individual). The ability of the market mechanism to accomplish this task (more or less strongly) depends on the following implicit assumptions.

5.2.3.1 Absence of Externalities

In earlier definitions, an externality was considered to be present whenever the utility function $U_i(.)$ of some economic agent i includes real variables whose values are chosen by another economic agent j without paying particular attention to the welfare effect on i's utility. As shown by Coase, the market mechanism may overcome some of these problems by adding "property rights" as tradable goods to the economy. Therefore an externality is nowadays said to be present whenever there is insufficient *incentive* for a potential market to be created for some good and the non-existence of this market leads to a *non-Pareto-optimum equilibrium*. So far, the absence of externalities is the only premise which network effect literature – as discussed above – is trying to relax.

5.2.3.2   Complete Rationality of the Homo Oeconomicus

Network effect literature often relies on the neo-classical assumption that all agents not only know their own action space and utility function, but likewise have a complete and realistic model of all the other agents' current allocation, action spaces and utility functions as well! In a pure neo-classical "exchange economy" this assumption may be relaxed, and even when we only bargain with our direct neighbors the decentralized exchange still leads to a unique and Pareto-optimum equilibrium, but unfortunately only if there are no network externalities or indivisibilities (see below). But for "real-world" individuals, parametric and strategic (or strategic and statistical (Williamson 1985)) uncertainty (Hayek 1937) imposes constitutional bounds (Hayek 1994, 171) to the knowledge their decisions can be based upon. In addition, heterogeneous institutional and structural environments influence the decisions of individual socio-economic actors.

Therefore research in the area of *New Institutional Economics* (Hodgson 1993) rejects this concept of complete rationality in favor of a "learning" individual and search-theoretical models of evolutionary systems. Equilibrium analysis models are replaced by models of the evolution process of the multi-agent system being examined, in which the optimal action of actor i at time t is modeled as a function of his individual knowledge at this point in time.

5.2.3.3   Exclusion Principle

Prices only lead to Pareto-optimal collective action in a multi-agent system if the exclusion principle applies to the goods to be exchanged i.e. unique possession and ownership exists, permitting consumption only to a single individual. When common use or free duplication of products is possible (as is the case for information products like software), the equilibrium price is zero (if there were no copyrights artificially restricting this duplication as an incentive to the producer).

5.2.3.4   Consumption Paradigm

Utility is drawn exclusively from consumption, i.e. the *destruction* of resources. The temporary possession of a good (like e.g. a piece of art or game software), which is sold to some other individual after a certain time, cannot be evaluated in the utility function. When extending the model to a multi-period economy, this inclusion becomes possible, but immediately destroys the validity of price coordination. For information products in particular the neo-classical notion of "consumption" (together with the exclusion principle mentioned above) poses a major obstacle to market coordination.

However, if not the consumption but the use of the resource becomes the center of attention, *property rights* lose their additional potential for generating utility compared to *usufruct rights*. The "Network Economics" of the Information Age needs to move from a *consumer*-oriented to a *user*-oriented discipline, in which the efficient solution of scheduling problems (*which resources* are used *when* in *which process?*) will turn out to be a critical success factor for the efficient creation of social welfare.

5.2.3.5   Separation of Consumers and Producers

The classification of economic actors into *consumers* and *producers* turns out to be problematic in a world which is replacing the classical notion of "work" more and more by freelance activities, thus "mixing" both concepts. In a "prosumer economy" one must not neglect the fact that human work does "flow out of the power plug socket" like energy; but humans represent discrete *renewable resource*, whose entire economic and "recovery process" must be synchronized efficiently with other individuals in the network.

5.2.3.6   Divisibility of Resources

One of the most extensive restrictions is certainly the neo-classical assumption of arbitrary divisibility of all goods, i.e. one must permit each apple to be cut into n pieces, sold separately. What may be acceptable for the apple is impossible for screws or information. Interestingly enough, in defense of equilibrium theory it is argued that the "rounding error" arising from unjustified acceptance of the divisibility assumption "washes out" for large quantities. While this may be true with screws, the argument breaks down at least for all goods for which the optimum quantity for an individual's use is close to one (e.g. automobiles, houses and all *information* goods). In the context of software it seems rather unrealistic to assume that one user wants to use more than one copy at the same time as well as only use parts of the program code.

5.2.3.7   Concave Utility Functions / No Complementarities

The orders of preference of the consumers for the bundles of goods must be representable by (strictly) concave, continuous utility functions. How far this assumption differs from reality becomes clear if one realizes that this does not allow for modeling complementary goods, although complementarities can be found in all areas from recipes (if one ingredient is not available in sufficient quantity, the cake cannot be baked) and service industries (if I'd like to spend a three weeks vacation on an island, the flights without the hotel are as worthless as the hotel without being able to book the flights) to information or software (if one does not know the concept of Pareto optimality and there is no definition provided, the fundamental theorems stated above are of no value to the reader). It is this problem of complementarity which renders the "market solution" of *scheduling* problems impossible: If a resource is needed for ten time slices in sequence, and the process is not preemptive (as with the hotel stay), buying the ten time slices in separate auctions leaves me with too high a risk of ending up with some slices missing.

5.2.3.8   Absence of Transaction Costs

Neo-classical economics do not consider transaction costs, i.e. costs which are incurred in the preparation or execution of the exchange process. In New Institutional Economics the effect of transaction costs is explicitly modeled and for example considered to be one reason for the emergence of companies which economize on transaction costs by being "islands of more centralized control" in a decentralized market.

5.2.4   Towards an Interdisciplinary Theory of Network Effects

5.2.4.1   The Modeling Power Required of an Interdisciplinary Theory of Network Effects

After the critique of economic network effect theory and the neo-classical paradigm in general the question arises of what requirements have to be met by an *interdisciplinary* theory of network effects, which allow us to integrate and explain the *social* and *economic* interaction of *human* actors and *automated agents* (e.g. software agents trading at the stock exchange or EDI systems which automate logistic processes).

- Modeling of knowledge and uncertainty / bounded rationality

The network effect theory must allow for modeling the knowledge of individual participants (human or automated) and uncertainty concerning this knowledge (in particular concerning the behavior and knowledge of other participants in the multi-actor system, which will be called "society" in what follows).

- Evolutionary System Dynamics

However, since assuming bounded rationality usually implies the impossibility of determining analytical (ex ante) results for an aggregated entity - such as a whole network consisting of individually deciding agents - in terms of the existence and/or efficiency of equilibria, having recourse to empirical and simulative approaches seems unavoidable.

Numerical simulations based upon interacting software agents can help us to acquire empirical evidence for such complex systems. Giving up complete rationality renders the system of interactions "unsolvable" by an analytical determination of equilibria and proof of their uniqueness. Therefore one must instead rely on the simulation of system dynamics and the analysis of the observed behavior of the simulation model

- Emergence of system components and links

The approach should also be able to model the emergence of *new* participants and their "death" in the evolution process (to model for example the establishment or dissolution of institutional participants) as well as the emergence and dissolution of new links between existing actors, i.e. allow for an evolution of network structure.

- Abolishment of convexity and divisibility assumptions

Since many of the decisions to be modeled will be *discrete* choices and exhibit interdependence with decisions made by other actors, convexity and divisibility assumptions are totally inadequate and thus have to be dropped (which is less problematic in a setting that has already given up all hope of analytical solvability).

- The Economics of Intermediation

To overcome the lack of normative results from traditional models, a new approach to a theory of network effects should consider institutional designs for managing network related dependencies between individual network actors. In this context, the role of intermediaries needs to be emphasized. Generally speaking, intermediaries can compile and/or reallocate the information necessary for coordinating dependencies between actors. In terms of the uncertainties inherent in novel technologies, intermediaries could contribute to solving the coordination problems associated with positive network effects. Quite contrary to the prominent hypothesis of disintermediation due to reduced transaction costs on markets, the benefits associated with IT such as decreasing communication and information processing costs appear to be available to intermediaries as well. Thus a new approach should integrate the analysis of intermediate coordination designs, essential data requirements and associated incentives problems for intermediaries in order to contribute to solving dependency issues which are problematic for markets.

6 Simulation Model of the Software Market

Most traditional approaches towards modeling phenomena of network effect markets as described in section 5 rely heavily on restrictive simplifications and face the problems outlined above. Thus, many of the phenomena observed under network effects might directly result from those assumptions rather than from the perceived scale property. An exception to this is Wiese (1990) who criticizes the simplifications of analytical models and develops a simulation model with the more realistic assumption of discrete parameters (e.g. participants, number of sold products and time) replacing the simplification of continuous parameters and marginal results of analytical models. Defining price, heterogeneity of preferences and one- or double-sided compatibility as parameters, his models allow for more complexity and a more detailed analysis of pricing and other marketing strategies. While this approach can be seen as a step in the right direction, once again network effects are modeled by installed base, thus neglecting the structural determinants of the market.

In the following, a simulation model of an agent-based computational economy will be developed which addresses some of the important requirements outlined above. Of course, on the one hand, not all of the deficiencies described are of relevance in the context of this work. For example, it is not an objective to analyze potential market failure in software markets, welfare implications, or the need for public intervention (e.g. discussed in Gröhn 1999, Thum 1995, Shapiro/Varian 1998, Liebowitz/Margolis 1999, Katz/Shapiro 1998). On the other hand, it will take further research efforts to resolve all of the general drawbacks of approaches that are based on the neoclassical paradigm. Nevertheless, the following model can be seen as a first step in the direction of developing an interdisciplinary framework for the modeling of software markets which deals with the relevant real world phenomena.

According to the requirements described above, the adoption decision is modeled discretely, meaning that it is not rational to buy or use more than one unit of the same product or even of different products in the same category. This is an assumption which makes sense especially for information goods like software or

116

telecommunication products. Confirmed by the empirical results, the network effects in the utility function are modeled only as being dependent on decision behavior of the direct communication network of the potential buyer and not on the installed base. This also pays tribute to the bounded rationality of real-world actors. Therefore, in contrast to the installed base of traditional models, a distinction is made between relevant and irrelevant network effects.

One main hypothesis is that the (macro) dynamics of software markets as multi-actor systems depend not only on the individual (micro) decisions of the participants but also on personal neighborhood structures reflecting the institutional patterns of networks. The influence of various determinants on the diffusion process of software products such as price, heterogeneity of preferences, and connectivity, centrality, and topology of networks will be tested.

6.1 Determinants of Diffusion Processes in Software Markets

Important benefits of information and communication software derive from the ability to exchange data or information between system components. Users can be seen as participants in communication networks within which it is fundamental that communication partners use compatible software standards and therefore coordinate the use of their individual technology (Buxmann/Weitzel/König 1999).

Analyzing existing approaches, it was shown that traditional economic diffusion models are not suitable for modeling software markets. Furthermore, the economic theory of positive *network externalities* focuses rather on the *installed base* of a given product than on the structural properties of the *personal* network which influences the individuals' decisions. In contrast, network analysis covers many structural properties, but does not itself adequately model the dynamics of diffusion processes when strong externalities exist. In the following, both approaches will be integrated into a simulation model.

Based on the empirical results and by using concepts from the area of *relational network models of the diffusion of innovations* (Valente 1995, see section 5.1.2), the structural determinants of diffusion processes in software markets can be identified.

A basic concept in network diffusion analysis is the *personal network exposure* which is a measure of how intensively an individual is exposed to an innovation, i.e. how many of his or her links directly lead to an adopter of a certain innovation. Besides the assumption of the installed base (which implies fully connected networks), this is exactly the basic assumption of positive network externalities, i.e. the likelihood of adoption gets higher with increasing personal network exposure. It will later be considered when modeling the buying decisions of individual consumers.

Network effects lead to intra-group pressure towards conformity, which has been proven for business networks (either within company groups or among independent business partners) by the empirical studies in section 3. This is analyzed in the literature by the concept of *group membership*. This determinant is especially relevant for innovations that are highly interdependent, such as electronic communications (Rice et al. 1990). Groups or clusters within a larger network are typically identified by a higher intra-group communication density or degree of interconnectedness (Richards 1995). The EDI case studies, for example, reveal that companies restructure their supply chain by intensifying relationships with partners that support the appropriate standard and by replacing others that do not. Taking centralized coordination into account, the Lufthansa standardization and migration rules also enforce group conformity (within and beyond borders of individual companies). Another result of high intra-group density is that the group and its participants are more resistant to influence from outside their own restricted set of communication partners (Dankowski 1986). This is an explanation of the phenomenon that even in networks with very strong network effects, such as EDI networks, various stable clusters of certain standards are found. This effect of course fades the higher the connectivity of the whole network becomes, since clusters converge to one large group of highly interconnected participants with high overall social pressure towards standardization.

Besides the collective pressure towards compatibility, some individual participants in networks might have a strong influence on the adoption decisions of many others. The concept of *opinion leadership* analyzes this constellation. The extraordinary status of opinion leaders can result from different circumstances. On the one hand an actor might influence others by power. The empirical results show that companies are often urged by important business partners to buy compatible software solutions (e.g. the case studies of 3Com, Karstadt, Heraeus). Also, a central coordinating unit might force or influence otherwise independent companies (in a group) towards conformity (e.g. cases of Deutsche Bank, Heraeus, Lufthansa). Additionally, opinion leadership can also be the result of a high number of nominations, i.e. incoming direct links from other participants, or, taking also indirect links into account, of a high centrality. This means that a central participant reaches others more easily, meaning that the number of links (distance) to others in the network is smaller. Automobile vendors are a common example for central actors in business networks. From a general perspective, vendors have a higher centrality since it is not very common for suppliers to communicate with each other (hierarchical supply networks).

These findings led to the identification of the structural determinants of the diffusion of innovation in software markets (and in many similar network effect markets) shown in Table 24. The right column also shows the corresponding parameters that will be used for the simulation model and which will be introduced in the following sections.

Table 24: Determinants of diffusion of innovations in software markets.

DETERMINANTS	PARAMETERS
costs	price
stand alone utility (functionality) of the products	heterogeneity of preferences
influence of communication partners	function of network effects
personal network exposure	number of direct links to adopters
intra-group pressure towards conformity	intra-group density, network topology (closeness)
opinion leadership (through power)	extent of influence (network effect on other participants)
opinion leadership (through structural position)	centrality
intensity of communication	connectivity

6.2   Basic Model

The basis of the simulation is a simple model of the buying decision in network effect markets. The terminology is similar to the model of Katz/Shapiro (1985), but the term will be interpreted differently. Let r denote the stand-alone utility of a software product (i.e. the willingness to pay even if no other users in the market exist) and $f(x)$ denote the additional network effect benefits (i.e. the value of the externality when x is the number of other adopters). For reasons of simplification it is assumed that all network participants have the same function $f(x)$, i.e. their evaluation of network benefits is identical. It is also assumed that the network effects increase linearly, i.e. $f(x)$ increases by a certain amount with every new user. The design of the simulation model will allow these assumptions to be relaxed in future research. The willingness to pay for a software product can then be described by the term $r+f(x)$. Let p be the price or the cost of a certain software product/solution, then a consumer buys the solution if $r+f(x)-p>0$. In case of v competing products in a market, the consumer buys the product with the maximum surplus in the case where this exceeds 0:

$$\max_{i \in \{1,...,v\}} \left\{ r_i + f(x_i) - p_i \right\}$$

(1)

If the surplus is negative for all i then no product is bought. Term (1) implies that only one product is used at the same time. This is a common assumption in many network effect models (e.g. Wiese 1990, 10). It also seems to make sense for the software market, since it would be rather unusual to buy and use two different software products with the same functionality (e.g. Microsoft Office and Lotus Smart Suite) at the same time (see also the discussion in section 5.2.3. and 5.2.4).

Unlike most of the existing models for markets with network effects, the following simulations are conducted by modeling the software market as a relational diffusion network. In such networks the buying decision is not influenced by the installed base within the whole network, but rather by the adoption decisions within the personal communication network. The significance of this for buying decisions can be simply demonstrated by the following example. Figure 42 shows the communication network environment of consumer A who wants to buy a software product that serves his or her individual needs.

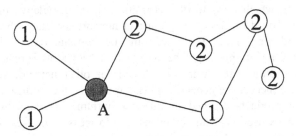

Figure 42: Communication network environment of consumer A.

There is a choice of two products (1 and 2) in the market. It is assumed that both products are free and have identical functionality, so that the buying decision depends only on the network effects. Applying traditional models that base the decision whether to adopt an innovation on the size of the installed base, consumer A would buy product 2 since the installed base with 4 existing adopters is larger. If the relational network approach is used and therefore the focus is only on the relevant communication partners of A, the consumer will decide to buy product 1 since the majority of the direct communication partners uses this solution.

Of course, this example is of a rather general nature. In the following, the importance of personal network structure will systematically be proven by conducting simulations. Additionally, it will be analyzed how varying the other determinants influences the diffusion processes of competing software.

6.3 Simulation Design

To determine the influence of the parameters on the diffusion process an analytical model would of course be favorable. For a given communication network and a specific constellation of the parameters the diffusion process, i.e. the interdependent behavior of the individual actors, the software market could theoretically be modeled as a Markov decision process. With a hypothetical number of 1,000 actors (used in the following simulations) and 10 products, it would consist of 10^{1000} possible states. Therefore, an analytical calculation of the transition probability and the stationary states of this process is not possible. A possible solution of this problem would be to limit the communication topology - and therefore the interaction in the network – to structures for which scalable analytical models about the collective behavior exist[9].

But since the major objective of this work is to determine the influence of communication topologies on the diffusion result, a limitation in this respect does not make sense, which leads to the necessity of using simulative methods. The simulations are based on the assumption that network structure, the consumers' preferences and the prices of the software are constant during the diffusion process. All the results presented below are based on a network size of 1,000 consumers. The simulations were also tested for other network sizes without significant difference in the general results. To analyze the diffusion process the distribution of products reached in this equilibrium was condensed into the Herfindahl[10] index used in industrial economics to measure market concentration (for an overview of different measures for market concentration and their advantages and disadvantages see Tirole 1993). All object types of the model were implemented in JAVA 1.1 and their behavior was simulated on a discrete event basis.

6.3.1 Network Structure

First, the $n=1,000$ consumers are randomly distributed on the unit square, i.e. their x- and y-coordinates get sampled from a uniform distribution over [0; 1]. In a second step, the network's structure is generated according to the parameters *connectivity*, *closeness*, and *centrality*. These parameters are introduced to analyze

---

[9]   Approaches of this kind can for example be found in the field of local interaction models of Game Theory. E.g. see Blume (1993) and Blume/Durlauf (2000) who build an analogy between social interaction and static mechanics to transfer the findings about aggregates of ferromagnetic atoms to aggregates of economic agents.

[10]   The Herfindahl index is calculated by adding up the squared market share for each vendor. If all market shares are evenly distributed among the ten alternative products, one gets the minimal concentration index of $10*(0.1)^2 = 0.1$ while one gets a maximal concentration index of $1*1^2+9*0^2 = 1$ if the diffusion process converges on all consumers using one identical software product.

the hypothesis that ceteris paribus (e.g. for the same network *size*) the *specific* neighborhood structure of the network strongly influences the diffusion processes.

In the following, the parameters are introduced.

connectivity $\in \{1;2;...;20\}$: The discrete number of direct communication partners (neighbors) attributed to each node (identical for all 1,000 consumers).

closeness $\in [0;1]$: The continuous probability that a given node gets his c direct neighbors assigned to be the c consumers geographically closest to the node at stake. With the probability (1- *closeness*) the direct neighbors are randomly selected. The extreme cases, i.e. all nodes get assigned either to the closest or to the random neighbors, are referred to as *close* topology or *random* topology, respectively.

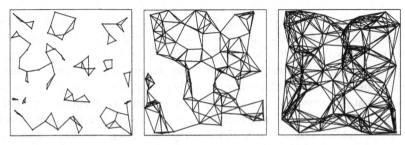

Figure 43: Typical networks with two, five or ten closest neighbors (close topology, i.e. closeness = 1.0).

The graphs in Figure 43 give examples of randomly sampled cases of the *close* topology (the example is of 100 consumers and a connectivity c of two, five and ten, respectively). It is obvious that a low number of neighbors may lead to a network structure which is not fully connected, i.e. its consumers can only experience network externalities within their local cluster. The standardization processes in individual clusters cannot diffuse to any consumer in a different cluster. These "sub-populations" evolve in total separation and it is therefore rather unlikely that all the isolated regions evolve to the same global standard. With increasing connectivity (five or ten neighbors), the chances that a network is not connected becomes rather small, i.e. every sub-group of consumers, agreeing on a specific product, may "convince" their direct neighbor clusters to join them. The "domino effects" might finally reach every consumer even in the most remote area of the network. However, the number of "dominos" that have to fall before a standard which emerged far away in a certain area of the network reaches the local environment of an actor and therefore influences the decision to adopt is typically much higher than in the corresponding graph with *random* topology. Speaking more formally, the average length of the shortest path connecting two arbitrarily chosen vertices of the graph (i.e. the number of neighbors you have to traverse) is smaller for the same connectivity if the graph has a random topology.

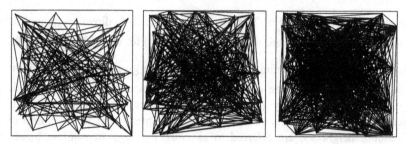

Figure 44: Typical networks with two, five or ten random neighbors (random topology, i.e. closeness = 0.0).

Figure 44 shows graphs with the same connectivity (2, 5, and 10) and the same number of consumers (100), but *random* topology. The optical impression of a higher connectivity (which is an illusion) results from the fact that "neighbors" were selected to represent an asymmetrical relationship. That is, when consumer x receives positive external effects from a neighbor y, it is unlikely in the *random* topology that vice versa, y also gets positive effects from x. Of course, within the *close* topology, symmetrical neighborhood is more common, meaning that there is a higher probability that if y is the closest neighbor from the perspective of x, at the same time x is also the closest neighbor from the perspective of y. In this case the two links are plotted on top of each other and that is why the close topology graphs look less connected.

Of course, most real-world networks represent an intermediate version of these extreme types, but since the costs of bridging geographic distance become less and less important the more information technology evolves, the tendency is clear. Electronic markets will resemble the *random* type of structure more (since partners are selected by criteria other than geographical distance), while in markets for physical goods (or face to face communication) physical proximity is still a very important factor for selecting business partners and therefore, the *close* topology will be a good proxy to the real world network structure.

centrality $\in [0;1]$: One can find various centrality measures in the network analysis literature (e.g. Freeman 1979, Freeman/Borgatti/White 1991). While these measures are useful for analyzing data sets of existing networks, they are not appropriate for a systematic generation of network topologies with different grades of centrality. Therefore, a new centrality parameter was developed for the simulations presented in the following. It allows to vary the centrality of network systematically. For calculating the c closest neighbors of node x, usually all nodes are sorted by ascending Euclidean distance $d(x, y)$. The centrality parameter biases this distance measure by calculating a weighted sum of the two nodes' Euclidean distance d(x, y) and the Euclidean distance d(y, *center*) of the target node y from the center (0.5; 0.5) of the unit square on which the nodes are plotted. The parameter *centrality* weights the two terms, which yields

$$(1 - centrality) * d(x, y) + centrality * d(y, center)$$

as the total term of the fictitious distance measure by which the list is sorted. If it is zero no "penalty" for off-center nodes is considered and direct neighbors are selected based only on local distance. However, when centrality is one, all c neighbors are selected to be the c most central ones, fully ignoring their own distance from this node. In this extreme case every node (except for the central nodes themselves) selects the same direct neighbors, yielding their "central role" as *opinion leaders*. Figure 45 demonstrates how the parameter *centrality* influences the network topology.

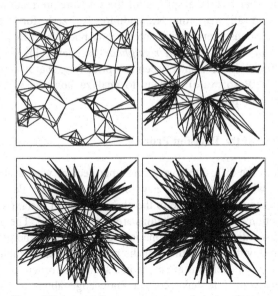

Figure 45: The effect of the centrality parameter on close topology graphs (25%, 50%, 75%, 100%).

6.3.2   Preferences, Prices, and Network Effects

Regardless of topology, in the simulation, every consumer can choose from all existing software products and knows all their prices. Initially, all consumers are (randomly) equipped with one software product, which may be considered to be their "legacy software" that is already installed and does not cause any further cost.

The direct utility that each consumer draws from the functionality of the *v* different products is then sampled from a uniform random distribution over the interval [0; *util*]. For each consumer and every software product the same interval was used. Thus, a value of *util*=0 leads to homogeneous direct preferences (of zero) while the higher the exogenously given value of *util*, the more heterogeneous the preferences of the consumers become (with respect to the different software products as well as with respect to the neighbors they communicate with).

The weight for the positive network externalities deriving from neighbors using the same software has been set to an arbitrary (but constant) value of 10,000 (for every consumer and every run).

In order to isolate the network externalities and heterogeneity of consumer preferences from other effects, all prices for the software products were fixed to a constant value and all marketing expenditures to zero for the simulations presented here, i.e. consumers decide solely upon potential differences of *direct utility* and the *adoption choices of their neighbors* (see term (1)). Nevertheless, the following simulations distinguish between low price (e.g. shareware products) and high price (e.g. ERP software) markets to analyze how the price level might influence the diffusion process.

6.3.3   Dynamics of the Decision Process

In each iteration of the diffusion, every consumer decides whether to keep his/her old software or whether to buy a new one based on the decision rationale described above (see term (1)). Due to the characteristic of instant scalability (see section 2) production or supply restrictions are not considered. The old software is assumed to be discarded once a new one is bought, i.e. it can neither provide the deciding consumer with direct utility nor the neighbors with positive externalities anymore. The adoption decisions are made in a sequential order, i.e. all consumers may always be assumed to have correct knowledge about the software their neighbors are currently running. Although a formal proof is not yet established, for the simulations this decision process always converges towards an equilibrium in which no actor will revise his decision anymore. No oscillation was found.

6.4 Results of Simulating the Diffusion Process

6.4.1 Low Price Markets

To analyze diffusion processes for low price markets a total number of 3,000 independent simulations were run with 1,000 consumers and 10 different software products until an equilibrium was reached. For every run all prices were fixed to the same constant value of $50 for all products. This means that switching to another software is very cheap compared to the positive externalities from neighbors (worth $10,000) if they use the same product. The distribution reached in the equilibrium was condensed into the Herfindahl index (described above). In the following diagrams, every small circle represents one observation (simulation run). Note that all the correlations illustrated in this work are significant on the 0.01 level.

The diagram in Figure 46 illustrates the strong correlation (0.756) of connectivity and equilibrium concentration for *close* topology (*closeness*=1.0). Despite this strong correlation, it can clearly be seen that even in networks with 200 neighbors per consumer (i.e. a connectivity of 200) the chances are still very low that one product will completely dominate the market. For *random* topologies (*closeness*=0.0) an even stronger correlation (0.781) is obtained (Figure 47).

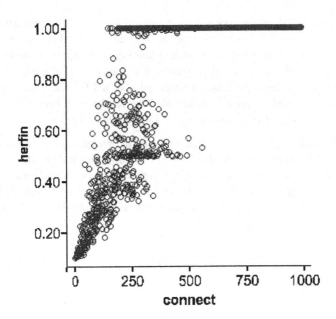

Figure 46: Strong correlation of connectivity and concentration for close topology (closeness = 1.0).

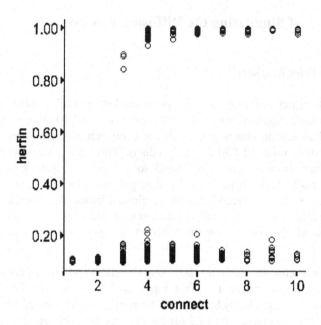

Figure 47: Strong correlation of connectivity and concentration for random topologies (closeness = 0.0).

Note that the scale of connectivity is extremely different in the two graphs of Figure 46 and Figure 47. It is obvious that the likelihood of total diffusion of only one software product is very high in a random topology network even for very low connectivity. Since the diagrams simply plot all circles on top of each other, the optical impression of the very frequent observation of a 1.0 concentration (in the top right corner of the graphs) is distorted. The results will become optically clearer in the 3-dimensional graphs of Figure 48 and Figure 49.

In Figure 48 and Figure 49 the *heterogeneity of preferences* is additionally considered in the analysis as a third dimension. No significant dependency of the sampled equilibria on this factor for *close* topologies was found (Figure 48). However, this changes if networks with *random* topologies are sampled (Figure 49). Here a slight but significant negative correlation of heterogeneity and concentration (-0.141) is found.

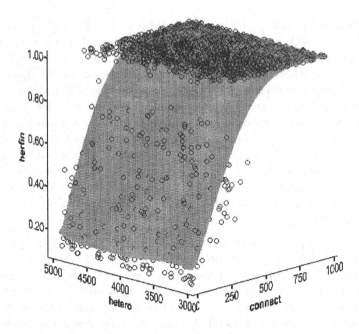

Figure 48: Equilibria in close topology (closeness = 1.0) networks.

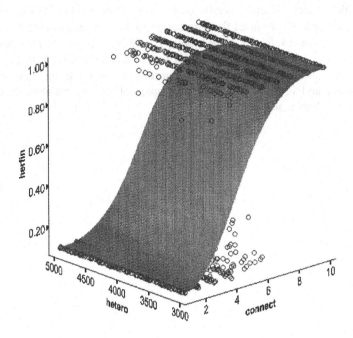

Figure 49: Equilibria in random topology (closeness = 0.0) networks.

Note that the axis for connectivity is again scaled from 1 to 10 neighbors in the diagram of Figure 49. It can clearly be seen that for 10 neighbors per consumer (1% of the total population) it is already almost certain that only one product will finally take over the whole market. Comparing this with the diagram of Figure 48 where the probability of reaching a concentration higher than 0.2 is almost zero for the same connectivity *strongly* supports the hypothesis that for a given connectivity the indirect domino effects are much stronger for *random* topology networks and thus the diffusion process shows much higher tendencies towards standardization. To test this statistically, a Kolmogorov-Smirnov test was run (Hartung 1989, 520-524) rejecting the hypothesis that the concentration indices obtained for close and random topologies follow the same distribution on a significance level better than 0.0005 (KS-Z of 2.261). This result substantiates the findings statistically.

A second interesting phenomenon can be seen in the fact that, although the mean concentration for a *random* topology networks of connectivity 5 is about 0.5, there are hardly any equilibria with concentration indices between 0.2 and 0.8, i.e. either the diffusion process leads to one strong product or many products will survive. This corresponds with the results of earlier analysis of standardization in fully connected networks (Buxmann 1996). In fact, the fully connected graph is equivalent to the concept of the *installed base* where a user of a certain product generates network effects for all other users of this product. This means that the findings of many approaches in the network effect literature, namely that in markets with network effects generally only one standard/product will dominate the market, is simply a result of the assumption of fully connected networks. In contrast to this, the results for *close* topology networks show that intermediate solutions with two or three strong products can be stable equilibria. This is obviously the result of sub-groups of consumers (with strong intra-group communication and fewer links to other groups) collectively resisting external pressure to switch their selected product.

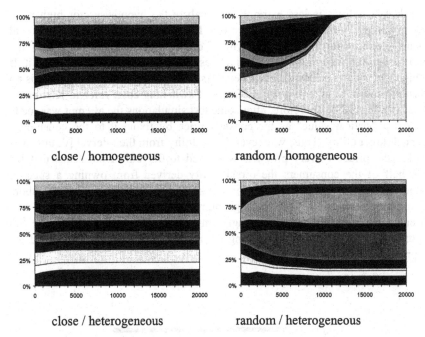

close / homogeneous   random / homogeneous

close / heterogeneous   random / heterogeneous

Figure 50: Typical diffusion processes for 1,000 consumers and connectivity of 5 depending on topology and heterogeneity of preferences.

Summarizing the findings so far, four typical patterns for diffusion processes towards an equilibrium depending on network topology and heterogeneity of preferences are displayed in Figure 50. The x-axis shows the number of iterations with every consumer deciding once per iteration. The y-axis illustrates the market shares of the 10 software products. Note that as discussed above the *random / heterogeneous* case is one of the rare intermediate cases (in Figure 49 it can be seen that there are hardly any equilibria for a connectivity of 5 and a concentration between 0.1 and 1.0).

The influence of topology on the diffusion of innovations in networks is obvious. While the *close* topology is generally the basis for a greater diversity of products since clusters or groups of consumers can be relatively independent from diffusion processes in the rest of the market, the *random* topology tends to market dominance of one or few products.

6.4.2 High Price Markets

Up to now, the simulation design might have been the correct model for competing shareware e-mail tools, or free internet-based phone or meeting software, but for many other software products the ratio of price to positive

130

network externalities is less extreme. To analyze the hypotheses for high price markets another 3,000 simulation were run. Increasing the prices (while this still remains identical for all products) will of course lead to higher inertia of the consumers towards buying a new product despite all of their neighbors using it. If too high a price was selected, everyone sticks to his initial solution and there is no diffusion process at all (on general effects of switching costs refer to Klemperer 1987a, 1987b, 1989). Therefore, after some test simulations the attempt was made to select a "critical value" as the constant price by fixing it to the consumer's expected direct utility. Thus, whenever direct utility from the interval [0; util] was sampled the price of every products was fixed to 0.5*util. This means that for about half of the consumers the direct utility derived from owning a specific product would not compensate for the costs as long as there are no neighbors yielding any network effects. The high number of processes that end in a low concentration equilibrium even for high connectivity (Figure 51 and Figure 52) supports this rationale when comparing the results to the processes obtained for low price software.

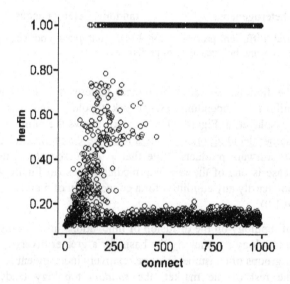

Figure 51: High prices lead to stronger inertia towards switching and less concentration for close topologies.

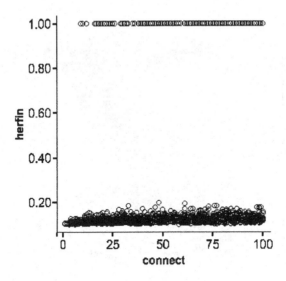

Figure 52: High prices lead to stronger inertia towards switching and less concentration for random topologies.

Note that in the graph of Figure 52 the x-axis only scales up to 100 neighbors. There are still more 1.0 concentration equilibria (total diffusion of one product) for *random* topologies than for *close* topologies. Nevertheless, even for *random* topologies the inertia effect is very strong. However, for both topologies there is still a significant positive correlation of connectivity and concentration (0.120 for *close* and 0.231 for *random*) although this is much weaker than for the low price markets. Please note again that the graphs of Figure 51 and Figure 52 display plots on top of each other resulting in optical distortion, which is resolved in the 3-dimensional graph in Figure 53 and Figure 54.

132

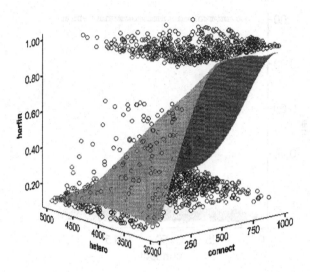

Figure 53: Equilibria in close topology networks for high price software.

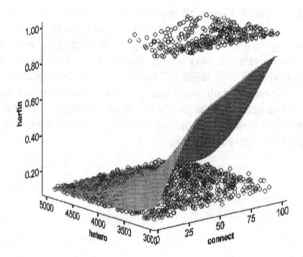

Figure 54: Equilibria in random topology networks for high price software.

Another very interesting effect can be observed if *heterogeneity of preferences* is additionally considered (Figure 53 and Figure 54). In contrast to low price markets, a much higher negative correlation is found, significant for both *close* (-0.611) and *random* (-0.500) topologies. Although higher heterogeneity has the positive effect of increased utility surplus for some consumers, others become even more reluctant to pay the high price, when there are no neighbors sharing this product as yet. Thus, they resist any domino effects much longer. Whether or not the domino effect may circumvent these resistant single nodes or clusters and still diffuse again depends heavily on the chosen network topology.

6.4.3 Varying Closeness and Centrality

So far, the influence of network topology on diffusion processes was analyzed only for the extreme cases of *close* and *random* topology with a closeness of 1 or 0, respectively. Another 10,000 independent simulation runs were conducted systematically varying the *closeness* parameter and additionally considering the *centrality* of networks. Complementing the parameter *closeness*, the „relative 2nd order radiality" was calculated, being the sum of the number of indirect neighbors of each node divided by the hypothetical maximum of indirect neighbors (if there were no double nominations by any direct neighbor). Of course this *radiality* measure correlates negatively with *closeness*. Therefore, a low *radiality* indicates dense intra-group links and thus resistance to outside pressure. The advantage of this measure is that it does not correspond to any auxiliary construction procedure like the arbitrary generated Euclidean distance used for the *closeness* parameter.

The equilibrium concentration was found to correlate positively with the two exogenous parameters *connectivity* (0.454), *centrality* (0.442), and *relative 2nd order radiality* (0.405) and negatively with *closeness* (-0.314). Although highly significant, the correlations themselves do not look as strong as one might have expected. A graphic illustration of the dependencies explains these results (Figure 55).

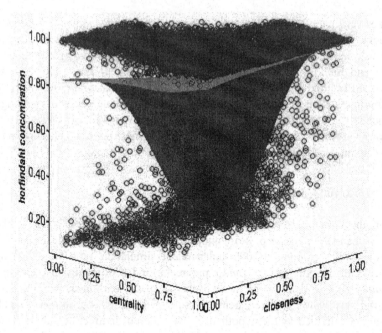

Figure 55: Joint impact of centrality and closeness on equilibrium concentration.

It can be seen from Figure 55 that for *close* topology and *low centrality* the result is almost certainly a low equilibrium concentration, i.e. multiple products survive, while increasing centrality or closeness fosters the concentration process. But one can also see that varying the centrality in a *random* topology (*closeness* = 0) has as low an impact on the concentration as varying *closeness* in a totally *centralized* (*centrality* = 1) topology. This explains the low univariate correlations (for example, the correlation of *concentration* and *centrality* rises to 0.864, when only those simulations that have a closeness > 0.9 are considered).

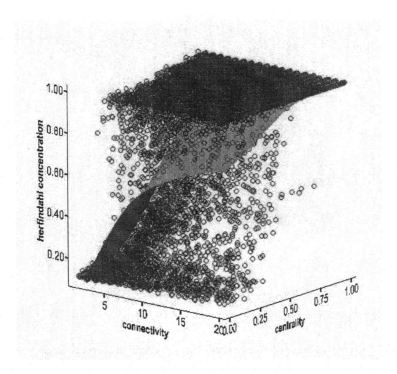

Figure 56. Joint impact of connectivity and centrality on equilibrium concentration.

For the interplay of *connectivity* and *centrality* the results are similar (Figure 56): In networks of *high centrality* even a *low connectivity* will not prevent the diffusion process from converging to a concentrated equilibrium.

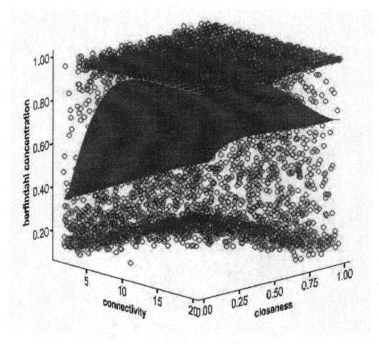

Figure 57. Joint impact of connectivity and closeness on equilibrium concentration.

For the joint effect of *connectivity* and *closeness* (Figure 57), this dominance is not quite as strong as in the other two cases: Even for *random topology* networks and networks with *high connectivity* the other parameter may still have a significant impact on the concentration.

6.4.4 Summary of the Results

Two separate simulations were conducted. In the first simulation the influence of the parameters *connectivity* and *heterogeneity of preferences* on the market concentration were measured for a *closeness* of 1.0 and a *closeness* of 0.0. A distinction was also made between low and high price segment. Table 25 and Table 26 show the results.

Table 25: Correlations between connectivity, and heterogeneity of preferences and market concentration in the low price segment.

LOW PRICE		
	Market concentration	
Connectivity	**0.756** (closeness = 1.0)	**0.781** (closeness = 0.0)
Heterogeneity of preferences	- (closeness = 1.0)	**–0.141** (closeness = 0.0)

Table 26: Correlations between connectivity, and heterogeneity of preferences and market concentration in the high price segment.

HIGH PRICE		
	Market concentration	
Connectivity	**0.120** (closeness = 1.0)	**0.231** (closeness = 0.0)
Heterogeneity of preferences	**–0.611** (closeness = 1.0)	**–0.500** (closeness = 0.0)

While in the first simulation the influence of *closeness* was only analyzed by its extremes of 0.0 and 1.0, respectively, this parameter was considered endogenously in the second simulation, again measuring its correlation with markets concentration. Also, the *centrality* of the communication network was taken into account. The influence of *connectivity*, *centrality*, and *closeness* (and as a complementing measure the radiality) were measured simultaneously. Table 27 shows the results.

Table 27: Correlations between connectivity, centrality, closeness, and radiality and market concentration.

	Market concentration
Connectivity	**0.454**
Centrality	**0.442**
Closeness	**–0.314**
Relative 2nd order radiality	**0.405**

The implications of the simulation results for software markets can be summarized as follows.

- *Connectivity* was used to model the source of *personal network exposure* within the diffusion process. It is shown to have a very strong positive influence on market concentration in the low price segment. This correlation weakens the higher the price segment.

- *Heterogeneity of preferences* was modeled by the stand-alone utility. Demand for variety leads to less concentration in high price markets for close and random topologies. In the low price segment, there is no significant dependency between heterogeneity and market concentration for close topologies, but a slight significant negative correlation for random topologies.

- The higher the *price segment* the more diversity of products is found due to the higher switching costs.

- *Closeness* was used to model Intra-group pressure. This parameter is shown to correlate negatively with concentration, meaning that although this pressure enforces group conformity, it also inhibits inter-group conformity. The influence of the network's *topology* on the diffusion of innovations in networks is obvious. While the *close* topology is generally the basis for a greater diversity of products (since clusters or groups of consumers may decide relatively independent from diffusion processes in the rest of the market), the *random* topology tends to dominance of one or few products.

- *Relative radiality* negatively correlates with closeness and therefore positively correlates with concentration. A low radiality can be interpreted as high intra-group pressure leading to intra-group or -cluster conformity and at the same time to inter-group heterogeneity.

- *Opinion leadership* (position and power) has been modeled by centrality and heterogeneity of node sizes (the latter was used to represent the strength of influence on others). The simulations show a positive correlation between centrality and concentration, showing that some central participants can significantly influence the diffusion process. Differences in power within the network did not have any effect on concentration unless it was combined with centrality.

By using a variation of the parameters closeness and centrality as an example, the results are demonstrated visually in Figure 58 to Figure 60. The nodes are the network participants and the edges show their communication relationships. Each software product is represented by a different color. The colors of the numbers show which product a certain node was initially equipped with. The colors of the nodes show the result of the diffusion process after equilibrium is reached.

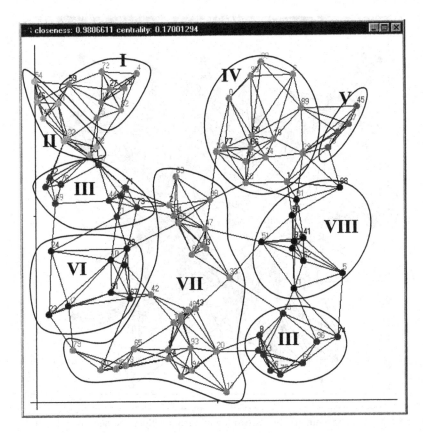

Figure 58: Market concentration in a network with high closeness and low centrality.

The different product clusters in Figure 58 are marked by the numbers I to VIII. It can clearly be seen that networks with a high closeness (0.98) are characterized by user clusters with a high inner-group density but only few links to external users. Combined with low centrality, this leads to a low market concentration, meaning that many different products survive in separate niches of the market. It is obvious that the high inner-group pressure towards standardization results in homogeneous use of software within the clusters while the influence between clusters is limited.

140

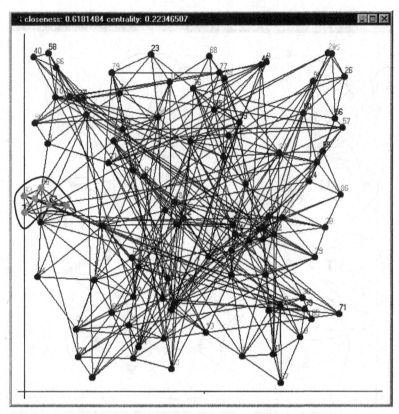

Figure 59: Market concentration in a network with medium closeness and low centrality.

Figure 59 shows a network with a comparably lower closeness of 0.62 and a higher centrality of 0.22. The market concentration is significantly higher, with only two products remaining in the market. Although one product dominates most of the market, another product has managed to survive in a stable cluster with densely interconnected users. While this phenomenon can be found in reality, most traditional models neglect this constellation (see 5.2).

Finally, Figure 60 illustrates the result of diffusion processes in a market with very low closeness (0.02) and relatively high centrality (0.41). As expected, the market ends up in a monopoly with only one software product dominating the entire market.

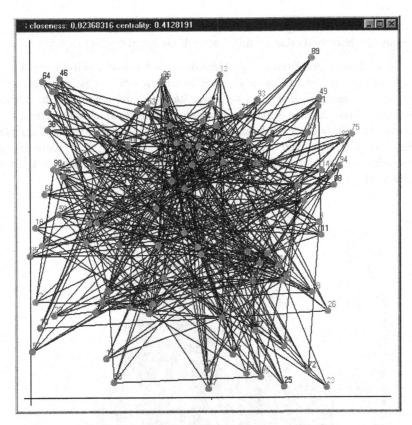

Figure 60: Market concentration in a market with low closeness and medium centrality.

These examples demonstrate how the simulation model is able to consider most different market constellations and explain a variety real world diffusion phenomena, which previously were only insufficiently covered in the models examined in section 4 and 5.

6.4.5 Annotations to the Parameter Design

Despite the strong impact of *centrality* and *closeness* on the diffusion process, one has to be aware of the fact that although the exogeneous parameters are sampled independently and thus do not correlate among each other, the *geographical* construction procedure is to some extent arbitrary and the two parameters *closeness* and *centrality* are parameters of this procedure rather than parameters of the resulting network *itself*. One could therefore argue that even though the geographical structure is "thrown away" after having generated the neighborhood relation and no further use is made of the nodes' location during the diffusion process, the results might only be generalizable to *geographic* networks since certain neighborhood relations might never be sampled by this procedure[11].

As a possible escape from this problem one could consider shifting the focus to exploring the *direct* explanatory power of the *structural* characteristics of the *networks* themselves, like e.g. its *average shortest path length*, on the diffusion process. Although, there is indeed a correlation of -.643, which is stronger than the correlation of any other single parameter, this escape is only partial: all structural characteristics that were tested systematically correlate with *closeness* and *centrality* and therefore certain combinations of these characteristics are never generated.

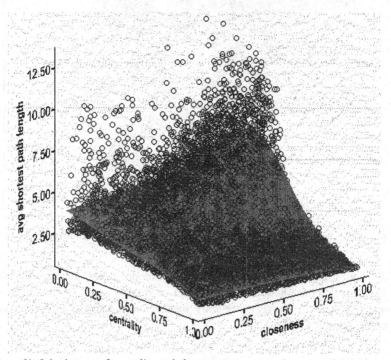

Figure 61: Joint impact of centrality and closeness on average shortest path length.

There are only two ways out of this dilemma: either collecting a large number of "real world" graphs (geographical and non-geographical) from different domains (see next section), and hoping that these samples are representative, or rather

---

11   For example, imagine the (admittedly fictitious) case that children tend to buy silverware compatible with that they are going to inherit from their parents: Thus the neighborhood relation is acyclic and exhibits "generation layers" having no intra-layer links at all. It is highly improbable that such a structure (or any other acyclic one) will ever be generated by the procedure in section 6.

"breeding" artificial graphs matching given target combinations of characteristics. Although this "breeding" is an NP-hard combinatorial optimization problem in most cases, some promising preliminary results were obtained with the application of simulated annealing (Kirkpatrick et al.1983). In section 8.2, first results of feasibility tests of the network breeding approach are presented. A method is developed to disclose real business networks from easily collectible data. Using computer simulations it can be shown that data from empirical studies designed to minimize complexity of the questionnaire for respondents can be used to find the real network structure and how the questionnaire's optimal complexity can be determined.

7 Marketing Implications

The market for software products has changed dramatically in recent years. Examples of this are fundamental paradigm shifts such as

- the shift from custom-made solutions to standardized products,

- the shift from DOS to operating systems with a GUI (e.g. Windows), and

- the shift from stand-alone solutions to networked systems.

Due to these dynamics, it seems difficult for the traditional marketing theory to keep up with the speed of development. Early[12] approaches tried to apply traditional marketing concepts to the specifics of software products and solutions. Some examples are the following publications. Based on empirical data and quantitative methods, Preiß (1992) identifies and evaluates strategic success factors for software companies such as quality and flexibility of the products, image of the vendor, or price. Gerhard (1992) analyses the German market for software by identifying the relevant characteristics of this industry. On the basis of his findings, he develops a framework for strategic and structural determinants in German software companies. Distinguishing custom-made software, standard software, and mass software Baaken and Launen (1993) identify strategic factors in software marketing, apply the traditional marketing instruments, and discuss a preventive policy for protection against competition. Wimmer and Bittner (1993) present marketing approaches for software from different authors covering very specific areas like strategic alliances, market research methods, software quality, or protection against software piracy.

Interestingly, the findings of network effect literature, which in some areas are highly relevant for software markets, are not sufficiently considered in all of these publications. Instead of systematically analyzing the determinants of the dynamics in software markets deriving from positive network effects and developing models

---

[12] Since this is a relatively young research field, *early* approaches are from the early nineties.

that are flexible enough to deal with this, the authors seem to stick with traditional marketing approaches and classifications.

In contrast to the publications that try to cover marketing theory as a whole and apply its instruments to software markets, one can find a large variety of publications in the field of network effects theory (see section 5.2) that focus on specific aspects or properties of network markets which can mostly be applied to the software market. Although these approaches add significant value to marketing literature in terms of developing strategies for vendors in network effect markets, they have certain weaknesses which were outlined above. Therefore, using the new approach of 6 two important marketing issues will be addressed in the following. Introducing a model for market classification and simulating competitive pricing strategies it will be demonstrated how the simulation model provides a solid foundation for developing a new marketing theory for software markets.

7.1 Classifying Software Markets

7.1.1 Classifications in Recent Literature: The Myth of Unstable Monopolies

The literature which considers positive network effects commonly classifies software markets by the two dimensions market concentration and stability (tippiness).

Many authors developed descriptive or analytical approaches to explain the phenomenon of tippiness and critical mass for network effect markets in general (see Wiese 1990 for a discussion and extension of the early approaches of Leibenstein 1950 and Rohlfs 1974; see Schoder 1995 for one of the most recent approaches). Based on the implicit or explicit assumption of indefinitely increasing and homogeneous positive network effects (see section 5.2.2) most of the authors agree that software markets tend towards monopolistic structures characterized by products with very large market shares. Besen and Farrell (1994) describe network markets as tippy by which they mean that the coexistence of incompatible products is unstable, resulting in one standard dominating the market. They also state that tipping can happen very rapidly. Arthur (1989, 1996) demonstrates that markets with network effects imply multiple equilibria and will finally lock-in to one technology which wins the whole market. Katz and Shapiro (1985) come to similar conclusions. Locking-in means that once a market tips toward a product or standard it may remain on that standard and its successors for a long time even if better products are available (Katz/Shapiro 1985, Farrell/Saloner 1985).

Recently, especially driven by the public discussion of the Microsoft antitrust case (Katz/Shapiro 1998), some researchers have reconsidered these findings. Two recent statements by well-known authors illustrate a new trend in the classification of software markets:

> "The industrial economy was populated with oligopolies: industries in which a few large firms dominated their markets. [...] In contrast, the information economy is populated by temporary monopolies. Hardware and software firms vie for dominance, knowing that today's leading technology or architectures will, more likely than not, be toppled in short order by an upstart with superior technology." (Shapiro/Varian 1998, 173)

> "Because bigger is better in increasing-returns industries, such industries tend to evolve into monopolies. Monopoly, however, does not lead inevitably to a bad economic outcome for society. [...] Sometimes an industry develops in such way, that monopoly is not only a likely outcome but also a desirable one. In such industries, what we are likely to witness is not conventional monopoly, but rather serial monopoly: one monopoly or near monopoly after another." (Liebowitz/Margolis 1999, 10)

In contrast to the approaches outlined above, the statements show that software markets are still seen to have a tendency towards a monopolistic structure, but at the same time the monopolies are unstable meaning that they do not lock-in to a certain technology once it is in the market. A vendor of new products can successfully enter the market (e.g. by aggressive marketing and/or a better product). The diffusion process will then end up in a new monopoly. At the same time Liebowitz and Margolis do not see any proof of the phenomenon of tipping, i.e. rapid diffusion of a technology that reaches a critical mass.

There are recent empirical studies by Liebowitz/Margolis (1999, 135-233) and Gröhn (1999, 109-114). Liebowitz and Margolis examine the markets for spreadsheets, word processors (see Figure 18 and Figure 20), office suites, personal finance software, desktop publishing (DTP) software, and browsers. In all of these, they find a tendency towards temporal (or serial) monopolies. With the exemption of personal finance and DTP software, Microsoft is the dominant vendor. Gröhn (1999) uses the concentration measure R_m[13] to aggregate the market shares of the $m=20$ world-wide largest PC software vendors (Figure 62).

---

[13]   This concentration measure simply adds the percentage of market shares α_i of the m largest vendors: $R_m := \sum_{i=1}^{m} \alpha_i$

148

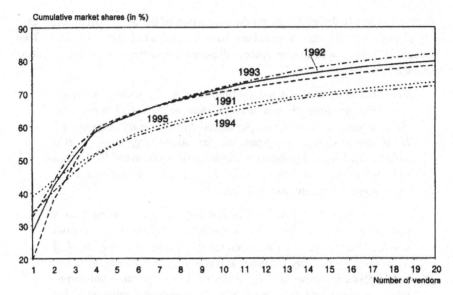

Figure 62: R_m concentration of the world-wide PC software industries (1991-1995).

The figure shows that the market share of the largest vendor (R_1) continuously increased from 23% in 1991 to about 40% in 1995. At the same time the gradient of the curves decreases especially in the beginning, where only a few vendors are taken into account. This means that the market leader was able to extend its dominance while at the same time, the market shares of its strongest competitors decreased. This increase in market concentration in the PC software market is contrary to the development in the IT industry as a whole. Here, the market share of the first 5 vendors decreased from over 50% in 1982 to 31% in 1994 (Gröhn 110). The reason for this is seen in the stronger demand-sided network effects in the software market. Interestingly, the market concentration differs between different types of PC software (Table 28).

Table 28: Market concentrations R_3 for different types of PC software (Gröhn 1999, 112).

Application	R_3 1995	Changes 1991-1995
PC Suite Software	100,00	0,00
PC Spreadsheet Software	95,34	3,21
PC Integrated Software	94,38	28,21
PC Personal Finance Software	84,81	31,30
PC Word Processing Software	80,15	12,87
PC Desktop Publishing	78,57	40,73
PC Graphics/ Draw and Paint Software	78,52	0,47
PC Desktop Database	77,80	6,15
PC Project Management Software	74,94	8,58
PC Accounting Software	68,30	21,45
PC Communication	66,79	15,58
PC Graphics/ Presentation Software	55,64	-10,40
PC Forms	53,84	-17,61
PC Utilities/ Application	47,41	-2,81
PC Information Management	36,35	--

Gröhn (1999) states that positive network effects are more relevant for some types of software products with high market concentration than for others with low concentration.

Liebowitz and Margolis (1999) and Gröhn (1999) use historical empirical data to hypothesize a correlation between the strength of network effects and market concentration. There is as yet no generic model yet to anticipate the market concentration and stability of products for which there is no empirical data (for example innovations like WebEDI). Furthermore, as shown in section 6, other relevant determinants might also explain the differences in market concentration. In the remainder of this section it will be shown how the empirical results of section 3 and the simulation results of section 6 might be integrated into a market classification of the three software markets this work focuses on. Implying different marketing strategies, typical market scenarios in terms of *concentration* and *stability* will be identified as well as typical vendor roles.

7.1.2 Market Scenarios and Vendor Roles

Table 29 summarizes the simulation results for the determinants that influence *market concentration* in the selected markets. As demonstrated, the determinants listed that are related to network structure (closeness, connectivity, centrality) are in fact the basis of a more detailed and differentiated analysis of network effects and their influence on market concentration (and stability).

Table 29: Determinants influencing market concentration.

	Influence on market concentration
Closeness	negative
Heterogeneity of preferences	negative
Price	negative
Connectivity	positive
Centrality	positive

Like market concentration, the determinants also influence *market stability*. The stability of a market in this context is the same as the speed of the processes of diffusion of innovations. The market is stable if the entry barriers are high or if a new product needs a long time to gain a significant market share. In contrast, the market is unstable or tippy, if a new product can quickly gain a significant market share or, in the extreme case, is able to take over the whole market. The literature (Shapiro/Varian 1998, 187-188, Katz/Shapiro 1994) has already discussed the fact that the demand for variety (in the simulation modeled as the heterogeneity of preferences) negatively, and the demand-side economies of scale (modeled as positive network effects in the utility function of each participant) positively influence the tippiness of software markets (see Table 30).

Table 30: Likelihood of market tipping to a single technology (Shapiro/Varian 1998, 188).

	Low economies of scale	*High economies of scale*
Low demand for variety	unlikely	high
High demand for variety	low	depends

Additionally, it is intuitively understandable, that *closeness, price segment*, and *connectivity* also determine stability (Table 31).

Table 31: Determinants influencing market stability.

	Influence on market stability
Closeness	positive
Heterogeneity of preferences	positive
Price	positive
Connectivity	negative
Centrality	positive/negative

Closeness was used to differentiate between networks with a different radiality. Networks with a low radiality (i.e. a high closeness) have dense communication clusters meaning that the choice of software products is determined by high inner-group pressure towards conformity, but is at the same time relatively independent of external influences. The existence of such clusters of course stabilizes the market, since it breaks the power of market-wide positive network effects and hinders the acceleration of gaining market share due to the critical mass phenomenon.

A higher *price segment* as well as higher implementation costs lead to a higher market stability, since these can be interpreted as switching costs leading to a less frequent change of solutions.

Low *connectivity* has the same effect, since the network effects experienced by individuals depend on their communication links to adopters of a certain solution. The fewer the links, the slower the diffusion process, and therefore the higher the stability of the market. Studies have empirically proved this positive correlation between connectivity of the whole network and speed of diffusion for other fields like medical, agricultural, and family planning innovations (Valente 1995, 42). In software markets one can expect this effect to be even more relevant due to the positive network effects which increase for a participant, the more communication links he has to other adopters (in the simulation model considered as *connectivity*). The extreme of a fully connected network therefore leads to the greatest instability. This explains why the traditional network effect approaches classify software markets as unstable: the consideration of the installed base of the whole market in every participant's utility function actually implies a fully connected network (see section 5.2).

As yet, no influence of *centrality* on the speed of diffusion processes in networks could be clearly identified. Empirical studies show different results for different kinds of innovations (Valente 1995, 52-54). As regards the selected software markets, the empirical studies of section 3 do not show a clear trend either. On the one hand, the central players in hierarchical networks are able to convince or force other participants towards a fast change to the desirable solution (see for example the case studies of Lufthansa, 3Com, Karstadt, or Deutsche Bank). On the other hand, this does not necessarily mean that the existence of such influential network participants has significant influence on the rest of the market (especially in markets with low *connectivity* and high *closeness*).

According to the empirical observations of section 3 and the simulation results of section 6 the software markets for ERP systems, EDI solutions, and office communication software can now be classified as follows (Figure 63).

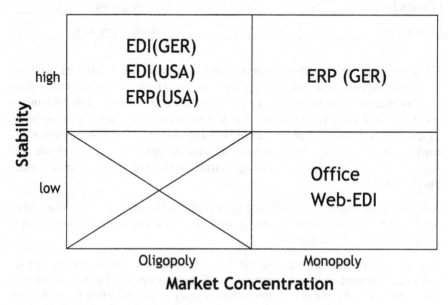

Figure 63: Scenarios for software markets.

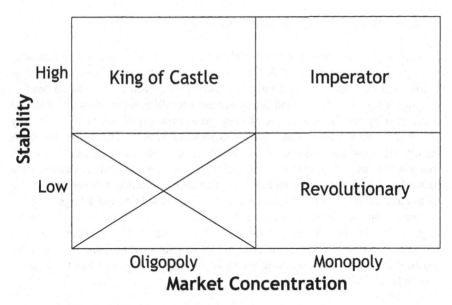

Figure 64: Typical vendor roles in software markets.

7.1.2.1 The Market for ERP Systems in the US

As shown in section 3 the *preferences* in the US market for ERP systems are heterogeneous. Individual companies have individual requirements. *Connectivity* is low since the focus is on compatibility within the company and not on communication between business partners. The case studies show that company groups can be seen as stable user clusters with high intra-group pressure towards standardization on the one hand and high resistance to external influences on the other hand. Therefore the *closeness* is high (or the relative radiality is low). The *price* segment is high, especially when costs for implementation and customizing are taken into account. According to the simulation model, this results in a stable oligopoly which, in fact, is found in reality (see Figure 15). Different vendors like SAP, Peoplesoft, Oracle Applications, or JD. Edwards gained stable market shares by developing the leading technology in specific segments of the market (e.g. for different industries or for different business processes). These vendors dominate a certain field within which it is very difficult for competing vendors to enter. Peoplesoft for example is known for its expertise in Human Resources solutions, Oracle Applications for order management systems, and JD. Edwards for solutions for medium enterprises and the chemical industry. Distinguishing typical roles of vendors in software markets, a vendor of this type shall be referred to as a *King of the Castle* (Figure 64).

7.1.2.2   Market for ERP Systems in Germany

In terms of the parameters of the model, the market for ERP systems in Germany is very similar to that in the USA. The *preferences* are heterogeneous, *connectivity* is low and the *closeness* is high as is the *price* segment. This should lead to heterogeneous user clusters and the opportunity for different vendors to survive in the market by specializing in one of these groups (niche). Nevertheless, in reality one finds a stable monopolistic market dominated by SAP. How does this make sense? As described above, the market is divided into various relatively independent user clusters due to different preferences and communication networks. A look at the real world reveals that SAP succeeded in entering many of these clusters (*castles*) by offering industry-specific modules and a large range of customization possibilities. This vendor's role is referred to as an *Imperator* (Figure 64). If the market persists in being clustered in heterogeneous user segments, it is very difficult for competitors to gain market share and push the *Imperator* out of its monopolistic position, since every segment has to be taken over independently.

7.1.2.3   Market for EDI Solutions in Germany

EDI solutions are based on EDI standards. The *preferences* for these standards are heterogeneous, since they cover different (e.g. industry-specific) requirements. *Connectivity* is rather low in Germany. The Fortune1000 survey revealed that 52% of the German responding companies use EDI technology with 21% of their business partners. The pressure towards conformity within the relevant business network is high (especially around strong players). The case studies show that large companies even restructure their supply and distribution networks in favor of partners that support the relevant EDI standard. Although one cannot directly infer a higher *closeness* in these emerging subnets, this leads to the same effects. Since the subnets dominated by a certain EDI standard have only few links between each other, resistance to external influence on the standardization decision is high. An analysis of the *costs* of implementing EDI solutions shows that the market belongs to the high *price* segment. The combination of these factors leads to a relatively stable situation in Germany in recent years with many different standards (see Figure 7). Whether this market constellation is going to change will be discussed later (see section 7.1.2.6).

7.1.2.4   The Market for EDI Solutions in the US

The market constellation for EDI solutions in the US is similar to that in Germany except for one parameter. *Connectivity* is significantly higher in the United States. The Fortune1000 survey shows that 75% of the companies that responded in the US use EDI technology with 38% of their business partners. As expected, this is reflected in the market concentration. While Germany has many different EDI standards, the two standards EDIFACT and ANSI X12 dominate the US market.

7.1.2.5   The Market for Office Communication Software

As shown by Liebowitz/Margolis (1999) the *preferences* in the market for office communication software are rather homogeneous. Although *connectivity* is rather low compared with the number of potential communication partners, it is obviously high enough (in combination with the low demand for variety and the low price) to lead to an unstable monopolistic market. Note that the positive influence of connectivity is much stronger in low than in high price markets. This is in fact the market structure which is referred to as a temporal or serial monopoly by Liebowitz/Margolis (1999) and Sharpiro/Varian (1998). As the example of Microsoft Office demonstrates, in these markets a superior product is likely to take over the whole market in a relatively short time. Because of this, a successful vendor is referred to as a *Revolutionary*.

7.1.2.6   The Emerging Market for Web-EDI

So far the classification of the respective markets was shown as a snapshot. Changes in market structures have not yet been analyzed. Using the example of the emerging technology of Web-based EDI it will be shown how such a dynamic can be examined on the basis of the new approach.

As described in section 3.2.2, the EDI market is in the process of change. In the past, EDI systems were dependent on one specific EDI standard. The standardization of products was limited due to incompatible in-house interfaces to which the solution had to be customized. In contrast, new web-based solutions with new technologies like XML promise to be flexible enough to support multiple standards embedded in standardized products (Weitzel/Buxmann/Westarp 2000). Therefore, preferences for individual EDI standards will lose importance. The new products will be far cheaper. Low costs and increased flexibility will reduce entry barriers to EDI networks, resulting in higher connectivity. While the incompatibility of EDI standards embedded in traditional solutions led to limited links between companies in different cluster-like EDI networks, such obstacles will disappear in the future resulting in joint networks of larger size. Traditional EDI networks based on a certain EDI standard will evolve to open networks with companies of every size and industry participating.

Taking these changes into account, it can be expected that the EDI market will move from a stable oligopoly to an unstable monopoly. Recent developments in this area seem to verify this hypothesis. Competitors like Ariba, Commerce One, Intershop, or Microsoft do not try to specialize in certain market segments. All of these companies try to gain significant market share with integrated and standardized solutions. Successful companies like Ariba or Intershop, starting as relative small companies with superior products, gained significant market share in Germany and the US much faster than one would expect when looking at diffusion processes in software markets in the past.

7.1.2.7 Managerial Guidelines for Kings, Imperators, and Revolutionaries

The more heterogeneous the preferences in the market and the more groups of users of a certain product are independent from external influences, the more likely is the market type to be a stable oligopoly. Here, typically, *Kings of the Castle* specialize in certain user groups with specific requirements relatively few user groups. The smaller the user cluster addressed and the more sophisticated the knowledge of the specific requirements of the relevant target group, the more stable is the position of the vendor. The primary objective of a newcomer has to be to identify such market niches which can be served with their own specific know-how. Since a smaller market is easier to overview, a good strategy for entering a certain segment can be to identify central players in the market and gain their trust in the solution. This strategy can be found in reality in the ERP market, where software vendors develop industry-specific products working close together with the largest companies, which then become the first customers. Penetration pricing is not a common strategy for *Kings of the Castle* since the number of potential customers is rather small compared to the entire market. Since the Unique Selling Proposition (USP) is the specific functionality of the product, customers are willing to pay a higher price than for products with higher standardization. The high price segment again adds to the stability of the market. A tendency to higher standardization, one of the ongoing paradigm shifts, is actually the biggest thread to vendors in stable oligopolistic software markets. The example of how traditional EDI might shift to WebEDI, a market which is likely to be an unstable monopoly, shows how traditional vendors come under great pressure, while newcomers experience enormous success with their standardized solutions.

One expansion strategy of *Kings*, that of leaving their *Castles* to build or conquer new ones, can be lucrative if their own market segment is safe and if large synergies with other segments can be identified. If the expansion is successful and large portions of the market can be taken over piece by piece, this is the strategy of an *Imperator*. The marketing implications are similar to the ones named above. The primary focus must be on the quality of the product. When entering segments of other vendors, penetration pricing might be the right strategy. Nevertheless, the example of Baan which came under extreme pressure in the ERP market, in spite of being much cheaper than their biggest competitor shows that pricing cannot compensate for lower quality. Again the biggest threat for *Imperators* in stable monopolistic software markets is a fundamental change in the market structure itself. In the market for ERP systems for example, one can identify an increased demand for standardization of the information and communication technology infrastructure throughout entire value chains, thus allowing data flows to cross industry boundaries. The higher the trend to standardization, the more the market moves towards instability. The recent poor figures of SAP and the fact that new software vendors are increasingly trying to enter the market might be the first sign of danger for the empire.

Revolutionaries (even when successful in monopolizing the market) live a dangerous life. Despite their high installed base, the market barriers are relatively low. Of course one could argue that the high fixed costs of producing the "first copy" of a software product are a significant entry barrier, but with the venture capital and stock markets becoming increasingly more flexible and sophisticated, there are many examples of the insignificance of such a barrier in modern software markets. Homogenous preferences and a low price segment result in unstable market conditions where superior innovations might take over the whole market in a short time. The fall of Netscape in the browser market is an example of a once successful *Revolutionary* which lost nearly their whole market to the competition. In 1996 Netscape had a market share of nearly 90% while Microsoft's Internet Explorer (IE) was far below 5% (Liebowitz/Margolis 1999, 222). Recent statistics show nearly the opposite proportion.[14] Two main reasons can be identified for this dramatic change. First, Microsoft improved its product until it became better than its competitor. An example of the superiority of the Internet Explorer is its early full support of XML, a new Internet data standard that gained great relevance (e.g. Weitzel/Buxmann/Westarp 2000), in early 1998. In contrast, Netscape released the first version of its browser with full support of XML as a preview release in the spring of 2000 (Navigator 6 Preview Release). In accordance with the findings of section 6, another reason for the enormous speed of the diffusion of Microsoft IE in the market is the high *connectivity* and a clear *random* topology (low *closeness*) of the Internet being the relevant communication network for the browser market. The implications for developing adequate marketing strategies in this type of market are clear. Monopolists have to be very aware of potential competitors since loss of market share can happen very rapidly. In markets where the relevant communication network has high *connectivity* and low *closeness* (such as the Internet) the threat is especially significant. Defensive strategies are constant product improvements (also giving the opportunity to continually charge existing customers) and decreasing prices (a strategy on which Microsoft's success in the office communication market is based, see Figure 19 and Figure 21). In contrast, newcomers have to consider the risks of market entry carefully. Despite the success story of Microsoft in the browser market (which was more of strategic relevance than to directly generate revenue, since the IE is free of charge), entering a software market of the *unstable monopoly* type can be

---

[14] According to StatMarket, usage of Internet Explorer has climbed steadily in the past 18 months from 64.60% on February 8th, 1999 to 86.08% on June 18, 2000. Netscape usage share has continued to freefall from 33.43% on February 9th, 1999 to 13.90% on June 18, 2000 (www.statmarket.com, 01.07.2000).

very costly and bears high risks of failure. In "winner-take-all, loser-gets-nothing" markets, one can find many examples of would-be revolutionaries ending up being guillotined by the force of the market.

7.2 Pricing in Software Markets

Positive network effects strongly influence the marketing strategies of vendors. Beside product policy, e.g. choosing the degree of compatibility with other products, communication policy, e.g. influencing the expectations of the future success of a network effect product, pricing strategy is most important for the success of software products. Generally speaking, pricing is of great importance at all stages of the product life cycle (Wiese 1990, 5-6). When introducing a product into the market, suppliers must convince potential early consumers to buy although they do not yet experience any positive network effects. Typically they do so by low prices which later increase with growing market share. But even when a critical mass of users has successfully been established, pricing remains a critical factor in building entry barriers against competitors, since modern network effect markets tend to be very dynamic.

In this section, it will be demonstrated that the diffusion of products in a network effect market not only varies with the set of pricing strategies chosen by competing vendors but also strongly depends on the *topological structure* of the customers' network. This stresses the inappropriateness of classical "installed base" models for the analysis of pricing strategies in software markets.

7.2.1 Literature Review

There are various approaches in economic literature that analyze the pricing of network effect goods. Estimating the hedonic price function, some authors prove the existence of network effects for products like computer hardware (Hartmann/Teece 1990), spreadsheet software (Gandal 1994, Brynjolfsson/ Kemerer 1996), database software (Moch 1995, Harhoff/Moch 1996), and word processing software (Gröhn 1999) and evaluate their influence on the market price empirically. The regression analysis shows that in network effect markets the price consumers are willing to pay is significantly higher if product characteristics enable compatibility and therefore generate network effects (Gröhn 1999, 115-136).

Focusing on optimum pricing in network effect markets, two strategies have been distinguished in the literature. *Personal price differentiation* means that network effect goods like software are sold to different user groups for a different price if the market allows such a separation. In the context of positive network effects the idea is to sell the product cheaper (or even giving it away free) to consumers with a low willingness to pay (students, pensioners) to increase the installed base. With growing market share and growing network effects, the sales of the product increase, generating revenue from groups with a higher willingness to pay, e.g. companies (Wiese 1990, Rohlfs 1974). This approach reflects the general assumption of most network effect models, namely that the installed base of the whole market and not the personal network of a consumer influences the individual buying decision. Apart from the fact that today's students might become full paying customers in the future, it is obvious that this assumption is unrealistic, since students will more likely communicate with other students and companies will more likely communicate within their business networks, thus devaluing the network effects of the other group. The implications of this aspect have already become clear in the simulations described above. *Dynamic pricing* is another strategy that is analyzed by many authors (Wiese 1990, Yang 1997, Klemperer 1987a, Clarke/Darrough/Heineke 1982, Katz/Shapiro 1994). Generally, an increasing price path is proposed for network effect goods, meaning that a new product is free or sold very cheaply at the beginning of its life cycle to gain an installed base large enough to overcome the start-up problem (*penetration pricing*). With increasing positive network effects and therefore higher willingness to pay, in later periods the price will be raised, generating sufficient revenue.

Taking the phenomenon of critical mass and the start-up problem into account, these pricing strategies are analyzed for vendors in monopolistic (Wiese 1990, Yang 1997, Clarke/Darrough/Heineke 1982, Dhebar/Oren 1985, 1986), or competitive environments (Wiese 1990, Katz/Shapiro 1996). Some authors also directly compare pricing strategies and their implications for different market types (monopoly, duopoly, oligopoly) (Economides/Himmelberg 1995, Wiese 1990).

Other prominent areas of interest, which will not be addressed in this work, are *pricing and licensing to competitors* (Economides 1996a), *pricing and switching costs* (Klemperer 1987a, 1987b), *pricing and timing of upgrades* (Thum 1995, Yang 1997), and *bundling strategies* (Bakos/Brynjolfsson 1999).

Most of the existing approaches use *equilibrium analysis* to analytically determine the results of pricing strategies in terms of market share. For an analysis of the basic assumptions and their deficiencies refer to section 5.2.

7.2.2 Simulation Design

The simulations of section 6 showed different results for high-price and low-price markets indicating that structural determinants might also be important for choosing the optimum pricing strategy in software markets.

Up to now all prices were fixed once, identical for all vendors and remained constant over all periods of the diffusion process. In the following, this assumption will be relaxed to explore the interplay of diffusion processes and the pricing strategies of the different vendors.

For reasons of computing time, the length of the diffusion process (which was twenty periods) was restricted to five periods, not really posing a restriction since most diffusion processes reached an equilibrium earlier than period five. The ten vendors are assumed not to be able to observe the prices of their competitors directly, but only the *reaction* of the customers, who react to their own pricing strategy by comparing the price and benefits of their products to those of their competitors.

In what follows, a *pricing strategy* is considered to be a vector of five discrete integer prices, one for each period, not restricted to being positive. Therefore, the possibility of subsidizing the use of a product in an early period (i.e. investing in a higher installed base) in order to "skim" the revenue from those who followed in later periods was not excluded.

For every set of ten price strategies, a specific diffusion process of a given network and thus a specific revenue (being equal to profit since no costs at the vendors' side are considered) was obtained for a given network topology for a given initial endowment and a specific order of decisions.

As before, a topology and initial endowment was sampled before running the diffusion process (for 1000 customers with connectivity of 10, centrality fixed to zero). In contrast to the simulations in section 6, this was not only done once but 10,000 times with different pricing strategies allowing the vendors to "learn how the market behaves" in response to their strategies and of course trying to find the strategy that maximizes their individual profit accounted for over the five periods.

At the start of the "pricing battle" all vendor have a constant price of 100 for each of the five periods. In the first simulated diffusion process this set of strategies yields a vector of 10 total profits. In each of the 10,000 diffusion runs another vendor is given the chance to adapt their pricing strategy in order to increase profit (in most cases at the expense of other vendors). This chance is taken by simply adding a random vector of five price "deltas" (drawn from a normal distribution) to the old strategy and then testing the new strategy by simulating a diffusion. Whenever the new strategy outperforms the old one or yields the same profit, the old strategy is replaced by the new one, otherwise the old one is kept and modified with another delta vector when it is this vendor's turn again.

Since all vendors exhibit this behavior, one might expect the "price battle" to lead to a Nash equilibrium, i.e. a set of price strategies, which makes it impossible for any vendor to improve his own profit when all other vendors stick to their current strategy. Unfortunately, although many battles reached an equilibrium in the sense that no vendor successfully tried to modify his strategy for some thousands of iterations, this does not mean that this equilibrium is a Nash equilibrium. There might still be a delta vector which simply has not yet been sampled and it is neither possible to enumerate all possibilities nor to analytically prove that such a superior strategy cannot exist, since the diffusion process may itself only be simulated. On the other hand, it might be possible to establish theorems, proving that under specific circumstances the negative effects of rising or lowering a price p in an early period may not be compensated for by any adaptation of prices in a later period, thus showing that p is part of a Nash equilibrium if (and only if) one can prove the same for all prices in consecutive periods (and all other vendors).

Nevertheless, the following figures, once again, show that the eqlibria resulting from this collective learning process lead to pricing strategies which again (indirectly) depend on the network's structure, influencing the customers' reactions to a given set of price strategies.

7.2.3   Simulation Results

One can see from Figure 65 that the total cumulative profit over all vendors (almost linearly with a correlation of -0.67) falls with the chosen closeness of the customers' network topology while, as expected, the total profit concentrates on fewer vendors in random topology markets than it does in close topology markets where many vendors survive with a substantial market share. Once again, the Herfindahl index is used to illustrate this concentration (Figure 66).

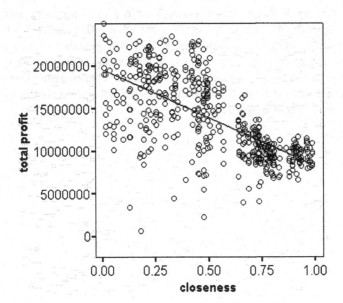

Figure 65: Sum total profit of all 10 vendors.

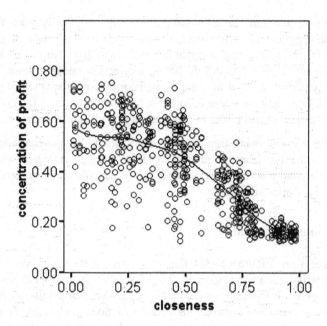

Figure 66: Concentration of total profit.

Although one might expect this to result from lower equilibrium prices in close topology markets, the following set of price charts (one for each of the five periods) clearly refutes this hypothesis: For all five periods the price *positively* correlates with topological closeness (with correlations of 0.23, 0.46, 0.76, 0.78 and 0.77 respectively). Since high closeness is one of characteristics that leads to a stable market, this substantiates the findings of the last section concerning pricing strategies for *Kings* or *Imperators*.

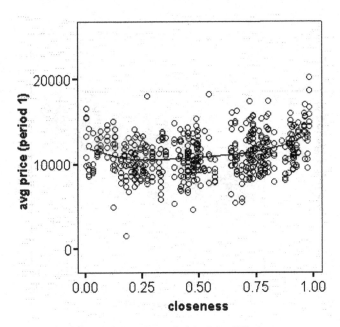

Figure 67: Average equilibrium prices for period 1 of the diffusion process.

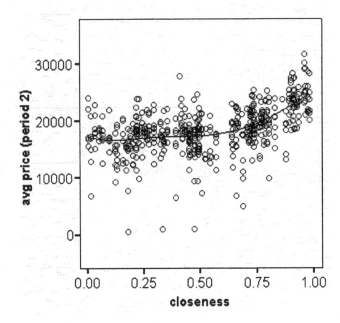

Figure 68: Average equilibrium prices for period 2 of the diffusion process.

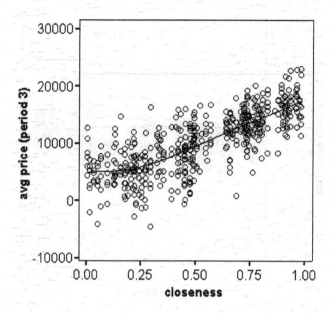

Figure 69: Average equilibrium prices for period 3 of the diffusion process.

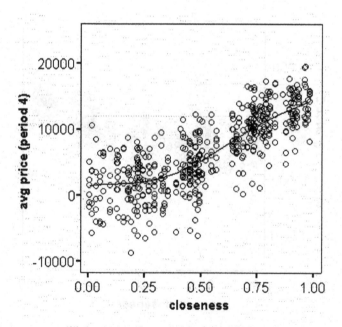

Figure 70: Average equilibrium prices for period 4 of the diffusion process.

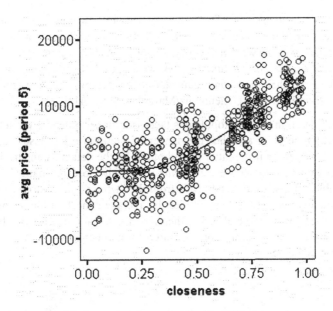

Figure 71: Average equilibrium prices for period 5 of the diffusion process.

Of course, if profits fall despite increases in prices, the answer lies in the *number* of customers buying the product: In close topology markets most customers only buy a product once, leading to stable clusters of local standards, while in the more "global" markets with random topology the first choice made to align ones own endowment with ones neighbors turns out to be erroneous, forcing me (and my neighbors) to buy a new product in a subsequent period (just as most owners of beta VCRs finally bought a VHS recorder too and owners of WordPerfect bought MS Word).

Therefore, on the one hand, in a close topology market vendors have the opportunity to behave like "local monopolists" (*Kings of Castle*), each of them with their stable groups of customers crystallizing, but in most cases only having one chance to charge them. For example, in the area of ERP systems there is an ongoing discussion whether SAP has enough potential of growing after the booming market in 1998 and 1999 when many large companies implemented an ERP solution to avoid the year 2000 problem (in European companies also for an easy switch to the new European currency). As a result, SAP is trying to enter the segment of small and medium sized companies. Of course, even in close topologies changing of software solutions can be common (especially in markets with homogeneous preferences and low prices) when large differences in functionality between different products occur. Describing their own experience with switching software after making wrong buying decisions, Liebowitz and Margolis illustrate that this situation can actually be common in real life. Starting with a platform transition from DOS and Atari ST to Windows, both

166

simultaneously decided to use AmiPro. They were unconcerned about the smaller markets share since the focus was on being compatible with each other, and they did not exchange files with many other people. A few years later, they both switched to WordPro due to functionality weaknesses of AmiPro. A week later they reconsidered their decision, again due to deficiencies of the software, and switched to Microsoft Word (Liebowitz/Margolis 1999, 141-143).

On the other hand, in random topologies there is a higher potential for selling, but also fiercer competition, and thus the danger of losing at least those "follow up" sales to the competitor if the latter turned out to be the defacto-standard in a later period. But nevertheless, those *Revolutionaries* "who lose the battle" may also derive a substantial share of total profit from the "wrong" initial decisions, which explains why even for random topologies the average concentration of total profit (over all periods) is only 0.6 although the market is taken over completely by one product and thus the concentration measured by number of users is 1.0 in those random topology cases.

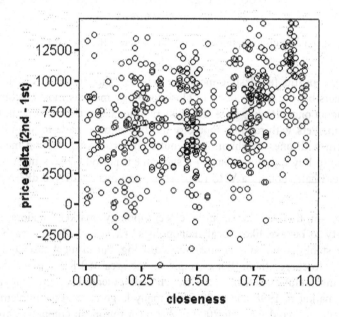

Figure 72: Concentration of total profit.

As one can see from the first two charts in Figure 67 to Figure 72 (the latter explicitly shows the price difference between the first two periods) *penetration* pricing indeed turns out to be the dominant strategy for all vendors, no matter whether the topology is close or random. But interestingly enough, although each "battle" was started with an initial price of 100, the vendors collectively (but without any chance of collusion!) raised this price to a much higher level of about 10,000. This is exactly the utility drawn from a neighboring consumer using the same product. Why this is a critical value becomes clear when one imagines a customer currently using product A and having e.g. three neighbors using the same product but four using product B (the remaining three neighbors using one or more other products): As long as the price of B is smaller than 10,000 the customer will be better off buying the new product, otherwise he or she will stick to A. Therefore, offering a price slightly below this threshold may in fact speed up the diffusion of a product. The fact that the average prices lie above the threshold is explained by the fact that once a vendor has to fight a competitor with a penetration strategy, it might turn out to be rational to "give up" the fight and select a skimming strategy by charging a higher price in the first period(s).

One can also see that after period 2 equilibrium prices fall again. That they may even fall below zero seems completely irrational for period five, since there is no future period in which such a subsidization could pay off. But since price changes are accepted as long as they yield the same (or a higher) profit, the vendors do not "notice" this, as long as there is no customer who actually switches to their product and thus "asks" for the subsidy, i.e. this can only happen when diffusion has reached an equilibrium in an earlier period.

The simulations have proved that the diffusion of products in a network effect market not only varies with the set of pricing strategies chosen by competing vendors, but also strongly depends on the topological structure of the customers' network. This stresses the inappropriateness of "installed base" models, which abstract from the topological structure of networks. Although competitive *prices* tend to be significantly *higher* in *close* topology markets, they lead to *lower total profit* and *lower concentration* of profit for these markets.

Despite these interesting results many questions remain open. It seems promising to conduct further research to answer the following questions:

- How can a given solution be proven to be a Nash equilibrium ?

- How do the strategies of (ex post) "winners" of the competition game differ from those of "losers" and what may the "losers" learn from this? (Simply copying the winners' strategy cannot make the losers better off since if it did, their current strategy would not be an equilibrium.)

8 Conclusions and Further Research

8.1 Conclusions

The objective of this work was to identify the relevant determinants of modern software markets and to incorporate these in a simulation model which provides the basis for an integrated theory of software markets and for managerial directions for software vendors to develop and implement strategies in a new economy.

In order to achieve this goal, a comprehensive empirical survey of the Fortune1000 companies was conducted in Germany and the US and complemented by case studies of individual enterprises. Besides giving an overview of corporate behavior concerning the choice, adoption and use of products in the markets for ERP systems, EDI solutions, and office communication software as well as a comparison of the three markets, typical determinants of adoption in software markets were identified. Besides price, heterogeneity of preferences, and compatibility (source of positive network effects), it was also found that structural characteristics of the individual communication network significantly influence diffusion processes in software markets.

Searching for appropriate instruments to model the relevant determinants, three research fields seemed to be promising. *Standardization models* model decisions on standards in communication networks and describe the influence of different coordination mechanisms on the degree of standardization. While the relevance of compatibility and the costs and benefits of standardization (the latter can be seen as the positive network effects) are considered, the focus is rather on modeling the individual's decision-making and the efficiency of centralized and decentralized coordination mechanisms than on dynamic processes in markets.

Network effect theory focuses on the installed base of a given product rather than on the structural properties of the individual communication network, implying fully connected networks. This highly unrealistic assumption leads to the fact that the models are insufficient to explain important phenomena of the software market like the coexistence of different software products despite strong network effects, small but stable clusters of users of a certain solution, although a competing product is dominating the rest of the market, or the phenomenon that strong players in communication networks force other participants to use a certain software.

In contrast, *models of network diffusion* cover many structural properties, but do not adequately consider the dynamics of the diffusion process itself when strong externalities exist.

Taking the empirical findings into account, useful concepts from the three research areas were integrated into a network simulation model for software markets. The simulations came to the following conclusions. While heterogeneity of preferences, high product prices and a decentralized, regional or sparse structure of the network prevent concentration, homogeneous preferences, low prices, high connectivity, a random "global" topology or a centralized structure of the network promote concentration towards a single software product. Additionally, taking the market stability into account, the relevant markets were classified and typical vendor roles identified. The markets for EDI solutions in Germany and in the US are stable oligopolies as is the market for ERP solutions in the US. A typical vendor role in these markets is the *King of the Castle*, who specializes on one segment, competing by better product functionality and not by price. The market of ERP systems in Germany is a stable monopoly with the *Imperator* as a typical vendor role. An *Imperator* has succeeded in taking over many of the heterogeneous user clusters which also characterized the stable oligopoly. Here, it is very difficult for competitors to gain market share and push the dominant vendor out of its monopolistic position, since every segment has to be taken over independently. The market for office communication software and the emerging market for WebEDI belong to the unstable monopolies, with the *Revolutionary* as the typical vendor role. These are "winner-takes-all loser-gets-nothing" markets with a high level of competition and sometimes very rapid changes in market shares.

To illustrate how the simulation model might be used to derive appropriate pricing strategies, additional simulations were conducted. The influence of network structure on the optimum pricing strategies of competing vendors could be proven. As expected, in markets with independent user clusters, one finds a tendency to higher prices. However, the profit in such markets is smaller for the vendors, because the clusters limit the potential number of buyers and because switching between different solutions is more unlikely. If one is losing market share in unstable monopolies, it might be sensible to switch to a skimming strategy, since one is likely to be totally driven off the market anyway.

8.2   Further Research

The introduced approach towards modeling software markets can be a starting point for further research about phenomena under network effects. While developing the model and conducting various simulations the following research directions appeared to be of notable interest.

- *Dynamic network structure*: Although the model considers the dynamic of adoption processes in software markets, the structure of the communication network that determines the buying decision is assumed to be static. Nevertheless, the EDI case studies demonstrate that characteristics of software (innovations) might also influence the choice of communication partners. Business networks get restructured and with WebEDI the communication networks might get larger and higher connected. While different types of networks have already been analyzed in this work, a future extension could be the consideration of an evolutionary network structure during diffusion processes. A recent theoretical approach which analyses the influence of IT innovations on supplier relationships might be helpful in this context (Weber 2000).

- *Intermediaries*: As described in section 4.3, in a specialized world with independent actors with individual requirements, intermediaries in communication networks might increasingly play an important role in software markets in the future. In contrast, with a tendency towards standardization and with increasing flexibility of information technology, intermediaries for pure data transformation might also lose relevance. More research is necessary on how intermediaries influence decisions about software products, before it can be decided whether it is promising to integrate intermediaries in the simulation approach.

- *Marketing strategies*: The first applications of the simulation model for developing appropriate marketing strategies for software vendors in a new economy have been demonstrated in this work. Additional areas of research in this context can be identified. Especially the role of product policy in terms of choosing an optimal degree of compatibility to competing products (e.g. Katz/Shapiro 1994) could be an interesting field of research. Since the networks of the simulation model are bi-directional graphs, scenarios of one-sided and two-sided compatibility of products might be considered.

- *Individual decision-making*: In terms of the simulation of pricing strategies, of course, optimizing one's individual pricing strategy by this type of "learning by simulating the market and simulating the competitors" may heavily depend on how well the customer's decision model reflects their real decision function. To further analyze the decision behavior of individuals and how a change in this influences market processes, it seems promising to further integrate the more subtle consideration of decision making among corporate actors as modeled in the decentralized standardization model (section 4.2). Two extensions seem to be of particular interest: Coordination designs applied in enterprises and the visibility of data upon which buying decisions are based.

- *Development of an interdisciplinary network theory*: In section 5, the drawbacks of network effect theory and the neo-classical paradigm have been described and the requirements for the development of an interdisciplinary network theory have shortly been addressed. Some of these have been realized in the model of this work, but many questions remain open. Especially, a further integration of approaches from the research fields New Institutional Economics, the evolutionary branch of Game Theory (Aumann/Hart 1994), and Agent-based Computational Economics (ACE) (Vriend 1996) can lead to an interdisciplinary theory for the new economy.

After generally analyzing the diffusion of software networks with different topologies, in the future the simulation model can also be a good basis for analyzing real world data concerning the diffusion of software products in specific communications networks (e.g. business networks). Some preliminary research has been conducted in the context of this work as to how empirical network data can be collected for this research question. The approach will shortly be described in what follows.

Quantitative network analysis has a long tradition in disciplines such as geography (e.g. Hagget/Cliff/Frey 1977), sociology (e.g. Jansen 1999), or economics (Economides 1996b). Generally, empirical data about social networks is collected by asking the participants about their relationships with other participants. Work in the area of diffusion analysis also simultaneously collects data about the social behavior in terms of adopting an innovation, in order to analyze interdependencies between behavior and the structural elements of the network. To collect network data is time-consuming and costly. First, the borders of the relevant network must be identified, then every participant has to reveal their connections to the others. It must be ensured the data is complete or at least representative, i.e. a sufficient number of participants must provide their data. In this context, researchers often experience obstacles since data about relationships between individuals or organizations is often seen as confidential. This also applies to the collection of data in business networks for analyzing the diffusion of software products. Therefore, new methods of data collection must be developed.

Based on the experience gained with conducting the Fortune1000 study, some preliminary research has been done in this area. The goal was to develop a method which allows the acquisition of the data of real world business networks without explicitly asking the companies for the names of their business partners (suppliers and customers). How can this be done? The basic idea is to ask only simple questions which are not confidential and then use the power of computer simulations to reconstruct the real network. Suitable questions are for example the following:

Table 32: Data collection for generating real world business networks.

Please estimate the number of your business partners dependent on their size!		
small	medium	large
Supplier _____	_____	_____
Customer _____	_____	_____

Please estimate the revenue with your business partners!		
> than $1 mil.	$0.5 - 1 mil.	< than $0.5 mil.
Supplier _____	_____	_____
Customer _____	_____	_____

Please estimate the number of transactions with your business partners!		
> 10.000 per month	5-10.000 per month	< 5.000 per month
Supplier _____	_____	_____
Customer _____	_____	_____

The answers can now be interpreted as restrictions which the hypothetical network has to fulfil simultaneously for all participants. First, an arbitrary supplier network of the participating companies (which are known by name and size) is generated, meaning that every company that has relationships with n suppliers and m customers will randomly be given connections to n and m randomly chosen suppliers and customers. Of course these business partners will most likely have different characteristics (e.g. number of transactions or revenue) from the correct (but still unknown) business partners. For example, the hypothetical network could show (4; 2; 4) as the distribution of small, medium, and large suppliers while the real one (taken from the answers) is (5; 3; 2). One can now calculate an error coefficient, e.g. aggregate square deviations (which would be 6 for the example), which can be added up for the whole network. Minimizing this error coefficient can be seen as a combinatorial optimization problem (probably np-complete). Testing showed that heuristic methods such as Cooperative Simulated Annealing (Wendt 1995) were able to find solutions with an error coefficient equal to 0 after a short period of calculating. For this, hypothetical "correct" networks were generated with 100 companies with a number of business partners ranging from 5 to 20. After this, a random network was generated which was then changed using Cooperative Simulated Annealing until an error term of 0 was reached. Unfortunately, generating a network which has the same distributions over all characteristics (in the following referred to as properties) as the "correct" network does not yet mean that the exact customer and supplier relationships have been found: The fewer the properties (i.e. questions like the ones in Table 32) considered when the data is collected and the less the granularity of these (i.e. number of categories per characteristic), the higher is the likelihood that a number of different networks exists which have the same distribution over all characteristics but completely differ in structure.

1000 simulations were conducted to test how many properties with what granularity are needed to calculate the correct real world network. The hypothetical networks generated which realized an error coefficient of 0 were compared with the real network. The differences between the hypothetical networks and the real one were measured and aggregated in another error term, dividing the number of wrong edges by the number of total edges. Figure 73 shows how this error term (*errel*) depends on the number of different questions (properties, *props*) and the number of their categories (granularity, *granul*).

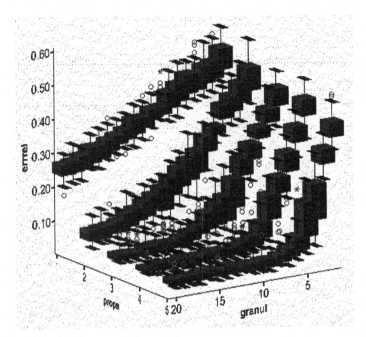

Figure 73: Quality of the generated networks.

The error term shown by the y axis shows the difference from the correct network. A value of 0 means that the exact right network was found. It can be seen that the correct business network could be calculated with the input of only 5 different questions with about 5 different categories to answer. Although the method is not yet sufficiently sophisticated, it is a good starting point for developing methods for collecting data about business networks.

References

Arthur, W. B. (1989): Competing technologies, increasing returns, and lock-in by historical events, in: The Economic Journal, 99 (March 1989), 116-131.

Arthur, W. B. (1996): Increasing returns and the new World of business, in: Harvard Business Review, 74 (July-August), 100-109.

Artle, R./Averous, C. (1973): The Telephone system as a public good: static and dynamic aspects, in: The Rand Jounal of Economics 4, 89-100.

Aumann, R. J./Hart S. (eds.) (1994): Handbook of Game Theory, Volume 2, Amsterdam (Elsevier).

Baaken, T./Launen, M. (1993): Software-Marketing, München.

Bakos, Y./Brynjolfsson, E. (1999): Bundling Information Goods: Pricing, Profits and Efficiency, Working Paper (1999), Stern School of Business, New York University, forthcoming in Management Science.

Balderston, F. E. (1958): Communication Networks in Intermediate Markets, in: Management Science, Vol. 4, 154-171.

Baligh, H.H./Richartz, L.E. (1967). An Analysis of Vertical Market Structures, in: Management Science, Vol 10, 667-689.

Bass, F. M. (1969): A New Product Growth for Model Consumer Durables, in: Management Science, Vol. 15, No. 5 (January 1969), 215-227.

Besen, S. M./Farrell, J. (1994): Choosing How to Compete: Strategies and Tactics in Standardization, in: Journal of Economic Perspectives, Vol. 8 (1994), No. 2, 117-131.

Blume, L. (1993): The Statistical Mechanics of Strategic Interaction, in: Games and Economic Behavior 5, 1993, 387-424.

Blume, L./Durlauf, S. (2000): The Interaction-Based Approach to Socioeconomic Behavior, forthcoming in: Durlauf, S./Young, H.P.: Social Dynamics; MIT and Brookings Institution Press.

Bolland, J. M. (1988): Sorting out centrality: An analysis of the performance of four centrality models in real and simulated networks, in: Social Networks, 10(3), 233-253.

Brynjolfsson, E./Kemerer C. F. (1996): Network Externalities in Microcomputer Software: An Econometric Analysis of the Spreadsheet Market, in: Management Science, vol. 42, Dec. 1996, 1627-1647.

Burt, R.S. (1987): Social contagion and innovation: Cohesion versus structural equivalence, in: American Journal of Sociology, 92, 1287-1335.

Buxmann, P. (1996). Standardisierung betrieblicher Informationssysteme, Wiesbaden.

Buxmann, P./König, W. (1998): Das Standardisierungsproblem: Ein ökonomisches Entscheidungsproblem zur Auswahl von Standards in betrieblichen Informationssystemen, in: Wirtschaftsinformatik 40, 1998, Heft 2, 122-129.

Buxmann, P./Weitzel, T./König, W. (1999): Auswirkung alternativer Koordinationsmechanismen auf die Auswahl von Kommunikationsstandards, in: Zeitschrift für Betriebswirtschaft, Ergänzungsheft 2/99, 133-151.

Buxmann, P./Weitzel, T./Westarp, F. v./König, W. (1999): The Standardization Problem – An Economic Analysis of Standards in Information Networks, in: Proceedings of the 1st IEEE Conference on Standardisation and Innovation in Information Technology SIIT '99, 1999, 157-162.

Ceci, S. J./Kain, E. L. (1982): Jumping on the bandwagon: The impact of attitude polls on polling behaviour, in: Public Opinion Quarterly 46, 228-242.

Church, J./Gandal, N. (1996): Strategic entry deterrence: Complementary products as installed base, in: European Journal of Political Economy, Vol. 12 (1996), 331-354.

Clarke, F. H./Darrough, M. N./Heineke, J. M. (1982): Optimal Pricing Policy in the Presence of Experience Effects, in: Journal of Business, Vol. 55, No. 4, 517-530.

Coleman, J.S./Menzel, H./Katz, E. (1957): The diffusion of an innovation among physicians, in: Sociometry, 20, 253-270.

Dankowski, J A. (1986): Interpersonal network structure and media use: A focus on radiality and non-mass media use, in: Gumpert, G./Cathcart (eds.), Intermedia, 3rd edition, New York, 168-175.

David, P. A. (1985): Clio and the economics of QWERTY, in: American Economic Review, Papers and Proceedings, Vol. 75, 332-337, 1985.

David, P. A./Greenstein, S. (1990): The economics of compatibility standards: An introduction to recent research, in: Economics of innovation and new technology 1, 3-41.

Dhebar, A./Oren, S. S. (1985): Optimal dynamic pricing for expanding networks, in: Marketing Science 4 (4), 336-351.

Dhebar, A./Oren, S. S. (1986): Dynamic nonlinear pricing in networks with interdependent demand, in: Operations Research 34 (3), 384-394.

Dybvig, P. H./Spatt C. H. (1983): Adaption externalities as public goods, in: Journal of Public Economics, Vol. 20 (1983), 231-247.

Economides, N. (1996a): Network Externalities, Complementarities, and Invitations to Enter, in: European Journal of Political Economy, Vol. 12, No. 2, 211-232.

Economides, N. (1996b): The Economics of Networks, in: International Journal of Industrial Organization, October 1996, 14, 669-71.

Economides, N./Himmelberg, C. (1995): Critical Mass and Network Size with Application to the US FAX Market, Discussion Paper EC-95-11, Stern School of Business, New York University.

Emmelhainz, M. A. (1993): EDI - A Total Management Guide, 2nd ed., New York.

Europäische Kommission (1997): Sicherheit und Vertrauen in elektronische Kommunikation. Ein Europäischer Rahmen für digitale Signaturen und Verschlüsselung, KOM (97) 503, Brüssel.

Farrell, J./Saloner, G. (1985): Standardization, compatibility, and innovation, in: Rand Journal of Economics, Spring 1985, 16, 70-83.

Farrell, J./Saloner, G. (1986): Installed Base and Compatibility: Innovation, Product Preannouncements, and Predation, in: The American Economic Review, Vol. 76, No. 5 (December 1986), 940-955.

Freeman, L. C. (1979): Centrality in social networks: Conceptional clarification, in: Social Networks, 1, 215-239.

Freeman, L. C./Borgatti, S. P./White, D. R. (1991): Centrality in valued graphs: A measure of betweenness based on network flow, in Social Networks 13 (1991), 141-154.

Gallaugher, J. M., Wang, Y. (1999): Network effects and the impact of free goods: an analysis of the web server market, in: International Journal of Eletronic Commerce 3 (4), 67-88.

Gandal, N. (1994): Hedonic price indexes for spreadsheets and empirical test for network-externalities, in: Rand Journal of Economics, Vol. 25 (1994), No. 1, 160-170.

Gerhardt, T. (1992): Strategie und Struktur in der deutschen Softwareindustrie. Eine industrieökonomische Untersuchung der Unternehmensentwicklung in der Softwarebranche, München.

Gierl, H. (1987): Die Erklärung der Diffusion technischer Produkte, Berlin.

Granovetter, M. (1978): Threshold Models of Collective Behavior, in: American Journal of Sociology, 83, 1420-1443.

Gröhn, A. (1996): Netzeffekte in der Software-Industrie: Eine Analyse der empirischen Literatur, Ein Modell der Netzeffekte in der Software-Industrie, Kieler Arbeitspapier Nr. 743, The Kiel Institute of World Economics, Kiel.

Gröhn, A. (1997): Ein Modell der Netzeffekte in der Software-Industrie, Kieler Arbeitspapier Nr. 790, The Kiel Institute of World Economics, Kiel.

Gröhn, A. (1999): Netzeffekte und Wettbewerbspolitik. Eine ökonomische Analyse des Softwaremarktes, Kieler Studien 296, Tübingen.

Haggett, P./Cliff, A. D./Frey, A. (1977): Location Models, Volume I and II, 2nd edition, London.

Harhoff D./Moch D. (1996): Price Indexes for PC Database Software and the Value of Code Compatibility, Discussion Paper 96-17, Zentrum für Europäische Wirtschaftsforschung (ZEW), Mannheim.

Hartmann, R. S./Teece, D. J. (1990): Product emulation strategies in the presence of reputation effects and network externalities: some evidence from the minicomputer industry, in: Economics of innovation and new technology, Vol. 1-2, 157-182.

Hartung, J. (1989): Statistik: Lehr- und Handbuch der angewandten Statistik, München.

Hayek, F. A. (1937): Economics and Knowledge, in: Economica, 4 (1937), 33-54.

Hayek, F. A. (1994): Rechtsordnung und Handelsordnung, in: Hayek, F. A. (1994): Freiburger Studien, Tübingen.

Hildenbrand, W./Kirman, A.P. (1976): Introduction to equilibrium analysis, North-Holland, Amsterdam, 1976.

Hodgson, G.M. (ed.) (1993): The Economics of Institutions, Hants (Edward Elgar Publishing) 1993.

Hogan, M. (1998): XML and the Internet: Driving the Future of EDI, February 1998, http://www.poet.com/PDF/XMLEDI.pdf.

Jansen, D. (1999): Einführung in die Netzwerkanalyse, Opladen.

Kansky, K. J. (1963): Structure of transportation networks: Relationships between network geometry and regional characteristics, Department of Geography, University of Chicago, Research Paper No. 84, Chicago.

Katz, M. L./Shapiro, C. (1985): Network Externalities, Competition, and Compatibility, in: The American Economic Review, Vol. 75 (3), 424-440.

Katz, M. L./Shapiro, C. (1986): Technology Adoption in the Presence of Network Externalities, in: Journal of Political Economy, Vol. 94 (1986), No. 4, 822-841.

Katz, M. L./Shapiro, C. (1992): Product Introduction with Network Externalities, in: Journal of Industrial Economics, 40 (1), 55-83.

Katz, M. L./Shapiro, C. (1994): Systems Competition and Network Effects, in: Journal of Economic Perspectives, Vol. 8, Spring 1994, 93-115.

Katz, M. L./Shapiro, C. (1998): Antitrust in Software Markets, Prepared for presentation at the Progress and Freedom Foundation conference, Competition, Convergence and the Microsoft Monopoly, February 5, 1998, http://www.haas.berkeley.edu/~shapiro/software.pdf.

Kindleberger, C. P. (1983): Standards as Public, Collective and Private Goods, in: KYKLOS, Vol. 36 (1983), 377- 396.

Kirkpatrick, S./Gelatt Jr. C. D./Vecchi M. P. (1983): Optimization by Simulated Annealing; Science 220 (1983), 671-680.

Kleinemeyer, J. (1998): Standardisierung zwischen Kooperation und Wettbewerb, Frankfurt.

Klemperer, P. (1987a): The competitiveness of markets with switching costs, in: Rand Journal of Economics, Vol. 18, No. 1, Spring 1987, 138-151.

Klemperer, P. (1987b): Markets with Consumer Switching Costs, in: The Quarterly Journal of Economics, May 1987, 375-393.

Klemperer, P. (1989): Price Wars Caused by Switching Costs, in: Review of Economic Studies 65 (1989), 405-420.

Leibenstein, H. (1950): Bandwagon, snob, and Veblen effects in the theory of consumers demand, in: Quarterly Journal of Economics, 64 (2), 183-207.

Levin, J./Fox, J. (1997): Elementary Statistics in Social Research, 7th edition, New York 1997.

Liebowitz, S. J./Margolis, S. E. (1994): Network Externality: An Uncommon Tragedy, in: The Journal of Economic Perspectives, Spring 1994, 133-150.

Liebowitz, S. J./Margolis, S. E. (1995): Path Dependence, Lock-In, and History, in: Journal of Law, Economics and Organization, April 1995, 11, 205-226.

Liebowitz, S. J./Margolis, S. E. (1999): Winners, Losers & Microsoft. Competition and Antitrust in High Technology, Oakland.

Lilien, G. L./Kotler, P. (1983): Marketing Decision Making. A Model Building Approach, New York.

Lufthansa Konzern-Informationsmanagement (1998a): Standardisierungsrichtlinien zur Informationstechnologie im Lufthansa-Konzern, Version 1.0, 1998.

Lufthansa Konzern-Informationsmanagement (1998b): Migrationsrichtlinien zu IT-Standards im Lufthansa-Konzern, Version 1.0, 1998.

Lufthansa Konzern-Informationsmanagement (1998c): Office-Konzeption 2000 für die Deutsche Lufthansa, Version 1.0, 03.12.1998.

Mahajan, V./Muller, E./Bass, F. M. (1990): New Product Diffusion Models in Marketing: A Review and Directions for Research, in: Journal of Marketing, Vol. 54 (January 1990), 1-26.

Mahajan, V./Peterson, A. P. (1985): Models for Innovation Diffusion, Sage Publications.

Marwell, G./Oliver, P./Prahl, R. (1988): Social Networks and Collective Action: A Theory of the Critical Mass, in: American Journal of Sociology, 94, 503-534.

Moch, D. (1995): Ein hedonischer Preisindex für PC-Datenbanksoftware: Eine empirische Untersuchung, in: Harhoff, D./Müller, M. (Hrsg.): Preismessung und technischer Fortschritt, Baden Baden.

Oren, S. S./Smith, S. A. (1981): Critical Mass and Tariff Structure in Electronic Communications Markets, in: Bell Journal of Economics, Autumn 1981, 12, 467-87.

Oren, S. S./Smith, S. A./Wilson, R. (1982): Nonlinear pricing in markets with interdependent demand., in: Marketing Science 1(3), 287-313.

Peat, B./Webber, D. (1997): XML/EDI - the E-business framework, August 1997, http://www.geocities.com/WallStreet/Floor/5815/startde.htm.

Preiß, F. J. (1992): Strategische Erfolgsfaktoren im Software Marketing: ein Konzept zur Erfassung und Gewichtung strategischer Erfolgsfaktoren mit Hilfe quantitativer Verfahren, Frankfurt.

Radner, R. (1992): Hierarchy: The economics of managing, in: Journal of economic literature, 30, 1382-1415.

Renn, C./Guptill, B. (1998): Distributed Computing Support: Where Does the Money Go?, in: Gartner Group: Research Note Strategic Planning Assumption, 29. April 1998.

Rice, R. E./Grant, A./Schmitz, J./Torobin, J. (1990): Individual and network influences on the adoption and perceived outcomes of electronic messaging, in: Social Networks, 12, 1-29.

Richards W. D. (1995): NEGOPY 4.30. A Manual and User's Guide, Department of Communication, Simon Fraser University, Vancouver, Canada, http://www.sfu.ca/~richards/negman98.pdf.

Rogers E. M./Beal, G. M. (1958): The Importance of Personal Influence in Adoption of Technological Changes, in: Social Forces, 36 (4), 329-334.

Rogers, E. M. (1983): Diffusion of Innovations, 3rd ed., New York.

Rogers, E. M./Shoemaker, F. F. (1971): Communication of Innovations, 2nd ed., New York.

Rohlfs, J. (1974): A theory of interdependent demand for a communications service, in: Bell Journal of Economics, 5 (1974), 16-37.

Schmacke, E. (Ed.) (1997): Die großen 500 auf einen Blick: Deutschlands Top-Unternehmen mit Anschriften, Umsätzen und Management, Neuwied et al.

Schoder, D. (1995): Erfolg und Mißerfolg telematischer Innovationen, Wiesbaden.

Segev, A./Porra, J./Roldan, M. (1997): Internet-Based EDI Strategy, working paper 97-WP-1021, http://haas.berkeley.edu/~citm/wp-1021.pdf.

Shapiro, C./Varian, H. R. (1998): Information rules: A strategic guide to network economy, Boston, Massachusetts.

Squire, L. (1973): Some aspects of optimal pricing for telecommunications, in: The BELL Journal of economics and management science 4, 515-525.

Thum, M. (1995): Netzeffekte, Standardisierung und staatlicher Regulierungsbedarf, Tübingen.

Tirole, J. (1993): The theory of industrial organization, 6th ed., Cambridge, Mass.

Tucker, M. (1997): EDI and the Net: A profitable partnering; in: Datamation, April 1997, http://www.datamation.com/PlugIn/issues/1997/april/04ecom.html.

Valente, T. W. (1995): Network Models of the Diffusion of Innovations, Hampton Press, Cresskill, NJ.

Vriend, N. (1996): Rational Behavior and Economic Theory, in: Journal of Economic Behavior and Organization 29 (1996), 263-285.

Weber, S. (2000): Information technology in supplier networks: A theoretical approach to decisions about information technology and supplier relationships, Frankfurt.

Weiber, R. (1993): Chaos: Das Ende der klassischen Diffusionsforschung?, in: Marketing ZFP, H. 1, 1993, 35-46.

Weitzel, T./Buxmann, P./Westarp, F. v. (2000): A communication architecture for the digital economy - 21st century EDI, in: Proceedings of the 33rd Hawaii International Conference on System Sciences (HICSS), 2000.

Weitzel, T./Son, S./Westarp, F. v./Buxmann, P./König, W. (2000): Wirtschaftlichkeitsanalyse von Kommunikationsstandards - eine Fallstudie am Beispiel von X.500 Directory Services mit der Siemens AG, SFB 403 Working Paper (00-05), J. W. Goethe-Universität, Frankfurt/Main.

Wendt, O. (1995): Naturanaloge Verfahren zur approximativen Lösung kombinatorischer Optimierungsprobleme - Integration von Simulated Annealing und Genetischen Algorithmen am Beipiel der Tourenplanung, Wiesbaden.

Westarp, F. v./Weber, S./Buxmann, P./König, W. (1997): Communication Services Supplied by Intermediaries in Information Networks: The EDI Example, in: SFB 403 Research Report (97-2), J. W. Goethe-Universität, Frankfurt/Main.

Westarp, F. v./Weitzel, T./Margaritis, K./Buxmann, P./König, W. (2000): Entscheidungen über betriebliche Standardsoftware - Die Migration des SAP-Systems bei der LSG, SFB 403 Working Paper (00-08), J. W. Goethe-Universität, Frankfurt/Main, http://www.vernetzung.de/eng/b3.

Wiese, H. (1990): Netzeffekte und Kompatibilität, Stuttgart.

Williamson, O. E. (1985): The Economic Institutions of Capitalism, New York et al.

Wimmer, F./Bittner, L. (1993): Software-Marketing: Grundlagen, Konzepte, Hintergründe, Wiesbaden.

WITSA (1998): Digital Planet. The Global Information Economy, Vol. 1, World Information Technology and Services Alliance (WITSA), http://www.witsa.org, Vienna.

Yang, Y. (1997): Essays on network effects, Dissertation, Department of Economics, Utah State University, Logan, Utah.

Appendix

Appendix A: Questionnaire

Johann Wolfgang Goethe-University Frankfurt am Main, Germany

Institute of Information Systems
Prof. Wolfgang König (koenig@wiwi.uni-frankfurt.de)
Dr. Peter Buxmann (buxmann@wiwi.uni-frankfurt.de)
Falk von Westarp (westarp@sims.berkeley.edu)

Empirical Survey about Standardization in Companies

We think it will take you approximately 20 minutes to fill out the questionnaire. Your answers will be kept absolutely confidential. Individual companies will not be identifiable in any of the reported results.

1. General questions about software products and standards in your company

1a. Please estimate how many different software products/standards are used in your company. If applicable, name the dominant product/standard.

	number	dominant product/standard
Office communication software (word processing, spreadsheet analysis, etc.)	___	_____
Database systems	___	_____
Software to support business processes (SAP, etc.)	___	_____
E-mail programs	___	_____
Network protocols	___	_____
Programming languages	___	_____
Operating systems	___	_____

1b.   What <u>advantages</u> do you see in central administration of software standards within your company?

	very important				un-important
• Guaranteed compatibility of different applications	☐	☐	☐	☐	☐
• Homogeneous systems are more flexible in case of changes	☐	☐	☐	☐	☐
• Economies of scale	☐	☐	☐	☐	☐
• Standardized design of programs reduces learning time of employees	☐	☐	☐	☐	☐
• Other _____	☐	☐	☐	☐	☐

1c.   What <u>disadvantages</u> do you see in central administration of software standards within your company?

	very important				un-important
• Employees best know what software they need for solving problems.	☐	☐	☐	☐	☐
• There are enough accessible interfaces to solve compatibility problems.	☐	☐	☐	☐	☐
• Trying to centrally specify software standards is doomed to failure anyways.	☐	☐	☐	☐	☐
• Other _____	☐	☐	☐	☐	☐

1d.   How sensible is <u>centrally specifying</u> common standards/software products in the following areas?

	very sensible				not very sensible
Office communication software (word processing, spreadsheet analysis, etc.)	☐	☐	☐	☐	☐
Database systems	☐	☐	☐	☐	☐
Software to support business processes (SAP, etc.)	☐	☐	☐	☐	☐
E-mail programs	☐	☐	☐	☐	☐
Network protocols	☐	☐	☐	☐	☐
Programming languages	☐	☐	☐	☐	☐
Operating systems	☐	☐	☐	☐	☐

1e.   How significant is the problem of incompatibility in your company in the following areas?

	very significant				very insignificant
Office communication software (word processing, spreadsheet analysis, etc.)	☐	☐	☐	☐	☐
Database systems	☐	☐	☐	☐	☐
Software to support business processes (SAP, etc.)	☐	☐	☐	☐	☐
E-mail programs	☐	☐	☐	☐	☐
Network protocols	☐	☐	☐	☐	☐
Programming languages	☐	☐	☐	☐	☐
Operating systems	☐	☐	☐	☐	☐

2. The use of software to support business processes

2a. Which of the following software products are used in your company to support business processes? (Please check all that apply).

- ☐ SAP R /2   ☐ SAP R/3   ☐ Baan-Triton   ☐ Peoplesoft   ☐ Oracle Applicat.
- ☐ J.D. Edwards   ☐ _____   ☐ _____   ☐ none

2b. The software solution to support business processes can contain standardized software (SAP, etc.) and custom-made software (that has been written exclusively for you).

Please estimate the proportion of standardized software in your company:

☐ 0-20%   ☐ 21-40%   ☐ 41-60%   ☐ 61-80%   ☐ 81-100%

2c. If you apply custom-made software, how was it predominantly written?

☐ in-house   ☐ outsourced   ☐ both equally

2d. How important are the following criteria for choosing certain software to support business processes?

	very important				un-important
• The functionality of the solution exactly fits our needs.	☐	☐	☐	☐	☐
• Our business partners predominantly use the same solution.	☐	☐	☐	☐	☐
• There are consulting services and complementary goods for this solution available on the open market.	☐	☐	☐	☐	☐
• The solution is currently in widespread use.	☐	☐	☐	☐	☐
• The solution is expected to be widespread in the future.	☐	☐	☐	☐	☐
• The solution is cheap.	☐	☐	☐	☐	☐
• Employees know how to use the solution.	☐	☐	☐	☐	☐
• Other _____	☐	☐	☐	☐	☐

2e. Who decides/should decide about the implementation of software to support business processes? (Please check all that apply).

	currently decides	should decide
• Company management	☐	☐
• Head/employee of the central MIS department (IT, IS, EDP, etc.)	☐	☐
• Head/employee of an operating department (e.g. controlling, production)	☐	☐
• Head/employee of a business unit	☐	☐
• Other _____	☐	☐

2f.	What is your opinion about software to support business processes?	I totally agree	I agree	indif-ferent	I dis-agree	I totally disagree
•	The share of standardized software relative to custom-made software will increase in my company.	☐	☐	☐	☐	☐
•	Custom-made software is mostly used to support critical success processes.	☐	☐	☐	☐	☐
•	In the future, so called "component-ware" (e.g. Java Beans) will substitute more and more for standardized software.	☐	☐	☐	☐	☐
•	In the future, standardized software will be easier to customize.	☐	☐	☐	☐	☐

3. The use of EDI

3a. Do you use EDI in your company?

☐ yes → please continue with question 3b.　　☐ no → please go to question 4.

3b. Why did you implement EDI?

	very important				un-important
• cost savings	☐	☐	☐	☐	☐
• time savings	☐	☐	☐	☐	☐
• to improve competitive position	☐	☐	☐	☐	☐
• to improve flexibility	☐	☐	☐	☐	☐
• to improve quality of business processes	☐	☐	☐	☐	☐
• requested by business partners	☐	☐	☐	☐	☐
• Other _____	☐	☐	☐	☐	☐

3c. Approx. how many business partners does your company have? _____

Approx. what percentage of your business partners do you use EDI with? _____%

Approx. what percentage of your total gross revenue is realized with these business partners? _____%

3d.	Which EDI solutions are used by your company? (Please check all that apply).					
	in use since (fill in year)	use is planned		in use since (fill in year)	use is planned
EDIFACT (and Subsets)		☐	DAKOSY		☐
ANSI X.12		☐	SEDAS		☐
VDA		☐	TRADACOMS		☐
SWIFT		☐	Others:_____		☐

3e. Why do you use this (these) particular EDI solution(s)?

	very important				un-important
The functionality of the solution exactly fits our needs.	☐	☐	☐	☐	☐
Our business partners predominantly use the same solution.	☐	☐	☐	☐	☐
There are consulting services and complementary goods for this solution available on the open market.	☐	☐	☐	☐	☐
The solution is currently in widespread use.	☐	☐	☐	☐	☐
The solution is expected to be widespread in the future.	☐	☐	☐	☐	☐
The solution is cheap.	☐	☐	☐	☐	☐
Other _____	☐	☐	☐	☐	☐

3f. To what extent are the following EDI services provided in-house or outsourced?

	exclusively provided in-house				exclusively outsourced
pure data transmission	☐	☐	☐	☐	☐
data security (authenticity, integrity, confidentiality)	☐	☐	☐	☐	☐
format transformation (from your format to the format of the business partner)	☐	☐	☐	☐	☐
format transformation (from the format of the business partner to your own format)	☐	☐	☐	☐	☐
Other _____	☐	☐	☐	☐	☐

3g. Please estimate the expenses of the company-wide <u>implementation</u> of your EDI solution!

- internal personnel time: _____ person-hours
- costs of software and hardware: $ _____
- costs of staff training: $ _____
- costs of external consulting services: $ _____
- other costs: _____ to the extent of $ _____

3h. Please estimate the annual cost <u>to run</u> the EDI solution company-wide!

- internal personnel costs for running and servicing the EDI solution: $ _____
- communication costs (telephone, network, etc.): $ _____
- annual expenses for EDI service provider: $ _____

3i. Please estimate the company-wide cost and time savings resulting from using the EDI solution!

- cost savings per year: $ _____
- time savings: _____ days per _____ (Example: *xxx* days per *order*).

3j. Who decides/should decide about the implementation of EDI solutions?
(Please check all that apply).

	currently decides	should decide
• Company management	☐	☐
• Head/employee of the central MIS department (IT, IS, EDP, etc.)	☐	☐
• Head/employee of an operating department (e.g. purchasing department)	☐	☐
• Head/employee of a business unit	☐	☐
• Other	☐	☐

3k. A new trend in the area of EDI is the use of the Internet to transfer structured business data (e.g. delivery notes, invoices).

In your company Internet-based EDI is

☐ already in use.   ☐ planned.   ☐ neither in use nor planned.

4. The use of office communication software

4. How important are the following criteria for choosing certain office communication software (word processing, spreadsheet analysis, etc.)

	very important				un-important
• The functionality of the solution exactly fits our needs.	☐	☐	☐	☐	☐
• Our business partners predominantly use the same solution.	☐	☐	☐	☐	☐
• There are consulting services and complementary goods for this solution available on the open market.	☐	☐	☐	☐	☐
• The solution is currently in widespread use.	☐	☐	☐	☐	☐
• The solution is expected to be widespread in the future.	☐	☐	☐	☐	☐
• The solution is cheap.	☐	☐	☐	☐	☐
• Employees know how to use the solution.	☐	☐	☐	☐	☐
• Other _____	☐	☐	☐	☐	☐

5. The use of internet technology

5a. Do you currently use/plan to use Internet technology, i.e. applications based upon TCP/IP? (Please check all that apply).

☐   No current/planned use

	currently	planned
• Individual employees do surf the WWW.	☐	☐
• We have a homepage.	☐	☐
• Internet-based solutions to link our suppliers and distributors	☐	☐
• Internet-based solutions to better serve our customers	☐	☐
• Intranet	☐	☐
• E-mail	☐	☐

5b.	The content and the presentation of information in the Intra/Internet is predominantly	for the Intranet	for the Internet
	administered by a central unit.	☐	☐
	administered decentrally (e.g. by the individual departments).	☐	☐

5c.	Data entry for the Intra/Internet is done predominantly	for the Intranet	for the Internet
	centrally.	☐	☐
	decentrally.	☐	☐

6. Your opinion

6. What is your opinion on following statements?

	I totally agree	I agree	indifferent	I disagree	I totally disagree
Standards/software products of the future will originate in the USA.	☐	☐	☐	☐	☐
I don't care which standards/software products others use, as long as everything runs smoothly in my company.	☐	☐	☐	☐	☐
My department should have the power to decide about company-wide implementation of standards.	☐	☐	☐	☐	☐
A lot of things could be better in my company if only the right standards were used.	☐	☐	☐	☐	☐
Because of increasing compatibility, changing between different standards is becoming easier.	☐	☐	☐	☐	☐
It is very difficult to reach an agreement with my company's business partners about using common standards.	☐	☐	☐	☐	☐

Still question 6. What is your opinion on following statements?

	I totally agree	I agree	indifferent	I disagree	I totally disagree
I am willing to accept functional deficits if the standard is widely established.	☐	☐	☐	☐	☐
I often think of practical improvements for the standards/software products we use.	☐	☐	☐	☐	☐
I would feel better if I could be independent from the mighty producers of standards/software.	☐	☐	☐	☐	☐
Prices of software products will significantely decrease.	☐	☐	☐	☐	☐
In the future plug-ins and the like will make widespread standards very customizable.	☐	☐	☐	☐	☐
Standards will no longer be so influenced by national boundaries.	☐	☐	☐	☐	☐
Software companies usually use low price strategies to establish a standard in the market.	☐	☐	☐	☐	☐

7. Questions about your company and you

7a. What is the size of your company?

- worldwide   revenues 1996: $ _____ (in millions)

                             employees: _____

- in the USA   revenues 1996: $ _____ (in millions)

                             employees: _____

7b. What industry are you in? _____

7c. What is your position and/or title? _____

We thank you very much for your help!

Appendix B: Questions of the Field Study on EDI over the Internet

1. When did you start using EDI OVER THE INTERNET [   ]

2. How do you primarily use the solution?
   a) Data entry through online forms [   ]
   b) Automated data exchange between two computer systems [   ]

3. Approx. how many business partner does your company use EDI OVER THE INTERNET with?
   a) customers [   ]
   b) suppliers [   ]

4. Please estimate the proportion of EDI OVER THE INTERNET in comparison to your complete EDI communication: [   ]%

5. What proportion do you expect in
   a) 2000 [   ] %
   b) 2005 [   ] %

6. The solution is based on standards software [   ]
   Please name the product(s): [   ]
   The solution is based on custom made software [   ]

List of Figures

196

198

List of Tables

List of Used Symbols

Symbols used in chapter 4

α	level of significance
c_{ij}	communication costs between the connected nodes i and j
$comcosts_{ijs}$	variable cost of the information flow along the edge between nodes i and j using a certain standard s
$E[c_{ij}]$	expected savings in information costs
$E[U(i)]$	expected utility for implementing a certain standard
F_{ijkls}	variable indicating the data flow transmitted from node k to node l passing through edge (i,j) and using standard s
$flow_{kl}$	amount of information transferred in the communication link between nodes k and l
i	index for network node
j	index for network node
p_{ij}	probability reflecting the believe of participant i that his communication partners j implement the same standard
K_i	standardization cost for node i
K_j	standardization cost for node j
k	index for network node
l	index for network node
μ	expected value
n	network size
s	index for standard
S	number of standards
σ	standard deviation
$stancosts_{is}$	costs incurring when node i is equipped with a standard s
t	index for standard
T_{iklst}	binary auxiliary variable for indicating whether in node i a flow of the communication link (k,l) is transformed from standard s into standard t (or vice versa)

$trancosts_{ist}$	variable costs resulting when an information flow is transmitted from a standard s to a standard t (or vice versa)
x_i	binary variable for node i (simple single period standardization problem)
X_{is}	binary variable for node i and standard s (extended single period standardization problem)
y_{ij}	binary variable, assuming the value 0 if two connected nodes i and j use the same standard
Y_{ijkls}	binary auxiliary variable for indicating whether a flow takes place along the edge (i,j) using standard s for the communication link (k,l)

Symbols used in chapter 5

a	innovation coefficient; network-independent benefits
A	technology
b	imitation coefficient
B	technology
D_a	density of an asymmetric network
D_s	density of a symmetric network
g_t	coefficient of diffusion
i	index for network participant
j	index for network participant
l	total number of consumers of x
M	cumulative number of potential adopters
n	network size
$n_{A,B}$	network effects determined by number of previous adopters of A or B
n^e	expected network size
N_t	number of adopters in period t
N^*_{t-1}	cumulative number of adopters until period $t-1$
P	price of network participation
q	consumption units

q_i	$\in [0; 1]$; 1 if (and only if) user i is part of a network
q_i^D	$\in [0; 1]$; 1 if (and only if) user i wishes to participate in network (demand)
r	willingness to pay without any associated network (stand-alone utility)
$rn_{A,B}$	network-related utility of actor of type R determined by $n_{A,B}$
η	individual
R	type of consumer preferring technology A over B
$sn_{A,B}$	network-related utility of actor of type S determined by $n_{A,B}$
s_i	state before action
s_j	state after action
S	type of consumer preferring technology B over A
t	index for time (period); index for consumer type
T	total number of existing links
$U_i(.)$	utility function
$v(y^e)$	expected value of network effect
$W(.)$	willingness to pay
x	network effect good
X	network size
x,y	specific allocations; network size
y	consumer
y^e	expected network size
Y	$\in [0; 1]$, set of t indices identifying users in a network
z_i	units of network effect good x

Symbols used in chapter 6

c	number of network neighbors (connectivity)
$d(x,y)$	Euclidean distance between node x and node y
$f(x)$	network effect benefits dependent on number of other adopters
i	index for software products
n	network size
p	price/cost of a certain software product
r	stand-alone utility of a software product
$util$	direct utility that each consumer draws from the functionality of a certain software product
v	number of different competing software products in a market

Symbols used in chapter 7

α_i	market share of vendor i
i	index for vendor
m	number of largest vendors
R_m	concentration measure of m largest vendors

List of Abbreviations

AM	Asset Management
ANSI	American National Standards Institute
B2B	Business-to-Business
CEFIC	Conseil Européen des Fédérations de l'Industrie Chemique
CO	Controlling
CSS	Cascading Style Sheets
DAKOSY	Datenkommunikationssystem
DIN	Deutsches Institut für Normung
DOS	Disk Operating System
DTP	Desktop Publishing
EANCOM	European Article Numbering Communication Association
EDI	Electronic Data Interchange
EDICON	Electronic Data Interchange Construction
EDIFACT	Electronic Data Interchange for Administration, Commerce and Transport
EDIFICE	Electronic Data Interchange Forum for Companies with Interests in Computing and Electronics
ERP	Enterprise Resource Planning
FI	Financial Accounting
FTP	File Transfer Protocol
GB	Gigabyte
GUI	Graphical User Interface
HR	Human Resources
HTML	Hypertext Markup Language
IDC	International Data Corporation
IM	Informationsmanagement

IS	Information Systems
ISO	International Organization for Standardization
IT	Information Technology
MB	Megabyte
MHz	Megahertz
MIS	Management of Information Systems
MM	Materials Management
NBü	Normenausschuss Bürowesen
ODETTE	Organization for Data Exchange by Teletransmission in Europe
OS	Operating System
PC	Personal Computer
PP	Production Planning and Control
QM	Quality Management
RAM	Random Access Memory
RINET	Reinsurance and Insurance Network
SD	Sales and Distribution
SEDAS	Standardregeln einheitlicher Datenaustauschsysteme
SMEs	Small and Medium Enterprises
SQL	Structured Query Language
SS	Spread sheet
SWIFT	Society for Worldwide Interbank Financial Telecommunications
TCO	Total Costs of Ownership
TCP/IP	Transmission Control Protocol / Internet Protocol
TRADACOMS	Trade Data Communications Standard
UN	United Nations
VAN	Value Added Network
VCR	Video Cassette Recorder
VDA	Verband der Automobilindustrie
VHS	Video Home System
W3C	World Wide Web Consortium
WP	Word processor
WWW	World Wide Web
XML	Extensible Markup Language